成都建筑·遗珠 I

Chengdu Architecture HERITAGE I

成都市规划管理局
成都市城市建设档案馆 编

成都建筑·遗珠 I

Chengdu Architecture HERITAGE Ⅰ

成都市规划管理局
成都市城市建设档案馆 编

遗珠

四川美术出版社

成都建筑·遗珠

CHENGDU
ARCHITECTURE
HERITAGE

成都市规划管理局
成都市城市建设档案馆 编

《成都建筑·遗珠Ⅰ》编辑委员会

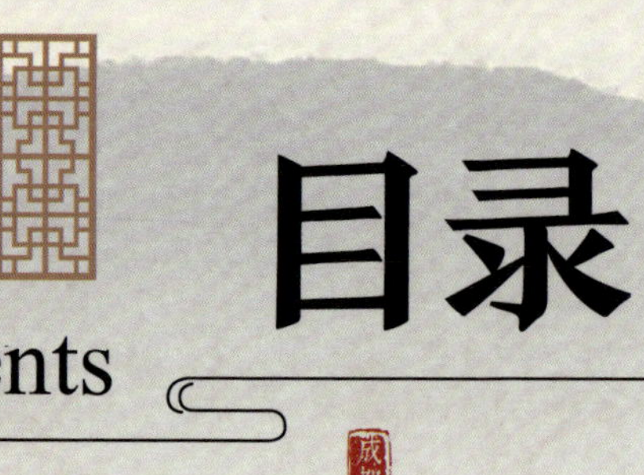

目录 Contents

都江堰南桥
South Bridge, Dujiangyan

九天开出一成都
万户千门入画图

——《上皇西巡南京歌十首》唐·李白

Chengdu, carved out by Heaven millions of years ago, presents before the eyes a picturesque view of myriad beautifully decorated households.

—*Retired Emperor Xuanzong Tours Chengdu*

By: Li Bai (Tang Dynasty)

序言
Preface

一座城市，它以文化为基，以历史为柱，以精神为顶。建筑是一座城市气质与美感的外化，朱雀雕梁，镌刻着曾经的美学与教化，街坊邻里，成为满足社交的温暖存在；建筑是历史的镜子，是记录城市发展年轮的载体，建筑不仅可以使用，更用事件、用理念、用故事在回溯历程时，致过去且敬未来，它可以提供城市记忆最生动、最形象的言说。它们是城市在沧桑岁月里光辉历史最宝贵的见证者，使城市的生命力得以在世代交替中延续。

成都有着4500年以上的城市文明史和2300多年的建城史，从宝墩遗址到开明王朝，从秦汉隋唐到新中国诞生，积淀了厚重的历史文化底蕴，是天府文化的创新性传承和创造性发展的中心地。川西先民尊崇天人合一的自然理念，依据“两江环抱、三城相重”的城市形态，结合本地气候、社会经济生活、民风民俗，发展出了独具一格的川西建筑形式。建筑造型轻盈精巧，布局灵活多变，与自然环境相映成趣，农耕文明的乡土气息格外浓郁，呈现出一种质朴的质感美、自然美，同时又契合成都人悠闲从容的生活节奏和包容创新的胸怀气度。

刘致平先生在《中国居住建筑简史》中写道：“清初各地移民入川，增加了文化的复杂性，于是四川住宅形制是非常丰富了。沿着移民路线兴建的祠堂、会馆，融入了历史、戏剧、宗教、儒学等诸多元素。两湖、客家等移民文化与土著文化相互交融，人口内迁以及随之而来的社会、经济吻合发展，使成都平原的建筑风格更是百花齐放，异彩纷呈。”

近代以来，受移民入川、教会传教、早期通商、民间传播等影响，成都的本土文化在与外来文化进行碰撞、交融的过程中，不断得到更新与发展。传统成都民居不断吸收外来的建筑文化，产生了丰富多样的建筑形态与类型，并在此基础上形成了适合当地的独特居住文化体系。传统与外来建筑之间的融合共同谱写了成都近代建筑的绚丽篇章。

改革开放40年来，中国的城市化进程以突飞猛进的形式改变着这片古老的土地，建筑在渐变中重生，在变化中传承。如何让情感记忆穿越历史，成为城市的魂？又如何让今天的城市风貌，给岁月以文明？改革开放并非要满溢新姿，更应该为城市留下“历史脚步”，从积淀中品鉴过去，思考未来，引导人民群众从历史建筑中读懂城市的珍贵记忆。随着《成都市历史建筑保护名录》的公布，成都保留下来的历史文化建筑遗珠重新进入大众的视野。

2018年2月，习近平总书记视察四川时，对成都工作给予充分肯定，明确提出“支持成都加快建设全面体现新发展理念的城市”，为成都未来发展指明了方向。基于这一认识，成都在实施新型城市化发展战略中，坚持激活更多本土文化资源，塑造具有本地文化特色的城市品牌，提升城市文化内涵，引领以文化振兴推动城市更新。

为更好地宣传成都作为全国十大古都之一和首批国家历史文化名城的独特魅力，弘扬中华文化，传承巴蜀文明，发展天府文化，助推成都建设世界文化名城，成都市规划管理局、成都市城市建设档案馆对成都市域现存历史建筑进行踩点、拍摄、梳理，策划推出《成都建筑·遗珠》系列画册，让历史建筑有机融入现代城市生活，为城市发展服务。今日我们对历史建筑的保护不仅仅是为了重现旧时风貌，更是为了明日城市的可持续发展。妥善保存城市的文脉，彰显“老成都，蜀都味，国际范”，使成都在走向现代化国际化的同时，不失自身独有的个性特色，保有自己独特的“味道”，这也是本书编纂的目的，是为序。

A city is based on culture, with history as the pillar and spirit as the roof. Architecture externally displays a city's temperament and sense of beauty. A rose finch decoration on a beam is engraved with the aesthetics and cultivation of the past; streets and neighborhoods are warm establishments to satisfy social contact; architecture is a mirror of history and a carrier for recording the development rings of the city. Buildings can not only be used, but also, with recalled events, concepts and stories, relate to the past and the future. It can provide the most vivid and visualized expressions of urban memories. Architecture is the most valuable witnesses of the glorious history of the city in the vicissitudes of life, so that the vitality of the city can continue over generations.

Blessed with a civilization history of more than 4,500 years and a city establishment history of over 2,300 years, from the Baodun Ruins to the Kaiming Dynasty, from Qin, Han, Sui and Tang dynasties to the birth of the People's Republic of China, Chengdu has accumulated a rich historical and cultural heritage and is the center of innovative inheritance and creative development of Tianfu Culture. Ancestors in the west of Sichuan Province revered the natural concept of unity of nature and mankind, and, based on the city form of "two rivers surrounding and three cities overlapping" and in combination with local climate, social and economic life, and folk customs, developed a unique form of West Sichuan architecture. Architectural forms are slim, graceful and exquisite, and the layout is flexible and varied, in harmony with the natural environment. The rural flavors of the agricultural civilization are extraordinarily rich, showing beauty of simple textures and nature and also combining the leisurely and relaxed lifestyle with moderate attitude of Chengdu dwellers.

Mr. Liu Zhiping notes in the book *A Brief History of Chinese Residential Architecture* that: "migrants entered Sichuan from across China in the early Qing Dynasty, adding to the cultural complexity, and thus shapes and structures of residential architecture in Sichuan were significantly enriched. Ancestral shrines and guild halls were built along the migration route, incorporating elements of history, drama, religion, and Confucianism, etc. Migrant cultures from Hunan and Hubei and the Hakkas were intermingled with the indigenous culture, and the migration inland and the subsequent social, economic and cultural development added extraordinary splendor to the increasingly diversified architectural styles of the Chengdu Plain."

In modern times, influenced by migrants' entry into Sichuan, church missions, early trade, and folk communication, the local culture of Chengdu has been continuously updated and developed in the process of colliding and blending with foreign cultures. Traditional Chengdu folk houses constantly absorb foreign architectural cultures, resulting in a variety of forms and types of buildings, and, on this basis, have formed a unique residential cultural system suitable for the local conditions. The integration of traditional and external architectures has written a brilliant chapter in Chengdu's modern architecture history.

Over the past four decades of reform and opening up, China's urbanization process has changed this ancient land in a rapid way. The architecture has been reborn through gradual changes and passed down amid changes. How can emotions and memories stand the test of history and become the soul of a city? And how can civilization be displayed in the current city appearances that has developed over years? Reform and opening up do not require totally fresh appearances, but leave "historical footsteps" for the city. Tasting the past and thinking about the future from accumulations, people should be guided to understand the precious memories of the city from historical buildings. As the List of Protected Historic Buildings in Chengdu is published, the historical and cultural building heritage retained in Chengdu has re-entered the public's vision.

In February 2018, when making an inspection tour in Sichuan Province, General Secretary Xi Jinping fully recognized the work of Chengdu and clearly stated that "support should be given to Chengdu to speed up the construction of a city that fully reflects the new development concept", pointing out the direction for the future development of Chengdu. Based on this understanding, in the implementation of the new urbanization development strategy, Chengdu insists on activating more local cultural resources, creating urban brands with local cultural characteristics, enhancing urban cultural connotations, and leading the promotion of urban renewal through cultural revitalization.

For the purposes of better publicizing Chengdu's unique charm of being one of China's top ten ancient capitals and one of the first national historical and cultural cities, promoting Chinese culture, inheriting Ba-Shu Civilization, developing Tianfu Culture, and driving Chengdu to build into a world famous cultural city, Chengdu Planning and Management Bureau and Chengdu City Construction Archives have surveyed, shot, sorted out, planned and launched the picture album series *Chengdu Architecture • Heritage*, so that historic buildings are organically blended into contemporary city life and serve city development. Our protection of historic buildings now aims not only to re-produce styles and features in the past, but also to properly preserve cultural elements of the city for its sustainable development in future and to manifest "Old Chengdu, Flavor of Sichuan Capital, and International Style", so that Chengdu, while going more modernized and international, does not lose its peculiar features and preserves its unique "flavor", which is also the aim of compiling this book. This is the preface.

章华里老宅院
Zhanghuali Old Courtyard House

前言
INTRODUCTION

金堂刁家祠堂
Diao's Ancestral Shrine in Jintang

前言 Introduction

成都，作为全国十大古都之一和首批国家历史文化名城，拥有丰厚的天府文化底蕴和广博的巴蜀文明积淀。建筑是"石头的史书"，历经时代沧桑变迁的历史建筑既是一份珍贵的建筑遗产，也是一位文化精神的见证者和承载者。成都的历史建筑，往往具有某一时代或若干时代叠加而形成的传统历史和文化价值，能够遗存下来显得弥足珍贵。

规划引领城市发展。随着近年成都经济的快速发展与城市建设的提档升级，成都市规划管理局着眼国家战略、区域发展和成都实际，为加快建设国家中心城市、美丽宜居公园城市、国际门户枢纽城市、世界文化名城做出了积极的探索。2004年成都市城市总体规划进行修编，确定了成都市历史文化名城保护体系规划。2005年底，《成都市优秀近现代建筑保护规划》正式出台，对原有历史遗产实施有效保护。2011年，成都市结合新版总体规划，编制了《成都市域历史文化保护和利用体系规划》，空间上，从"名城保护"拓展到"全域保护"；时间上，从"古代"延伸至"近现代"；对象上，从"文物古迹"拓展到物质与非物质文化遗产。

为贯彻落实中央新型城镇化工作会议和中央城市工作会议精神，成都市规划管理局组织开展了《成都建筑·遗珠》系列画册的编撰工作。通过系统梳理"成都记忆"的线索与载体，以历史文脉为主线，挖掘各个时期的建筑代表，串联整合后形成集中展示，全面彰显城市个性，重塑延续不断的城市记忆体系。画册以成都市人民政府公布的《成都市历史建筑保护名录》为内容，《成都建筑·遗珠Ⅰ》为第一卷，共收录了成都市50处历史建筑，生动捕捉这些历史建筑历经沧桑而风采依旧的真实面貌，追索着历史建筑承载的百年历史和人文情怀，展示着城市发展从追求生产价值转向生活价值、从经济导向转向人本导向的轨迹。

本书的出版，是秉承"历史文化是城市灵魂"的城市人文观，挖掘城市记忆，加强人们对历史建筑的整体认识，拓展历史文化保护的宽度和深度，弘扬中华传统文化，创新发展巴蜀文化。让这悠久的历史积淀支撑起成都市规划建设的新时代构想，历经光阴不改颜色。

As one of China's top ten ancient capitals and one of the first national historical and cultural cities, Chengdu has been blessed with abundant connotations of Tianfu Culture and profound accumulation of Ba-Shu Civilization. Architecture is "historical records with stones". Historic buildings that have undergone the vicissitudes of the times are both a precious architectural heritage and a witness and carrier of cultural spirit. Historic buildings in Chengdu are often characterized by traditional history and cultural value developed over a certain era or several eras, and their survival seems to be highly precious.

Planning goes ahead of city development. With the rapid economic development and upgrading of city construction in Chengdu in recent years, Chengdu Planning and Management Bureau, with an eye to national strategy, regional development and the real situation in Chengdu, has made active explorations for accelerating the building of national central cities and world famous cultural city. Chengdu's overall city plan was edited in 2004, determining the plan of protection system of famous historic and cultural city in Chengdu. In late 2005, the *Protection Plan for Excellent Modern and Contemporary Buildings in Chengdu* was formally issued for effectively protecting existing historic heritage. In 2011, with reference to the new master plan, Chengdu compiled the *Plan of Regional History and Culture Protection and Utilization System of Chengdu*, which, at the level of space, expanded from "protection of the famous city" to "full-dimensional protection", at the level of time, from "ancient" to "modern and contemporary", and, at the level of objects, from "historical and ancient sites" to tangible and intangible cultural heritage.

For the purpose of implementing the spirit of Central Work Conference on New Urbanization and Central Urban Work Conference, Chengdu Planning and Management Bureau has organized the compilation of the series of pictures albums of *Chengdu Architecture • Heritage*. Through systematic review of the clues and carriers of "Chengdu Memory", and with historical contexts as the main line, they have explored the architectural representatives of each period, and linked and integrated them in display, fully demonstrating the urban personality and re-creating the continuous urban memory system. The albums feature the contents of the *List of Protected Historic Buildings in Chengdu* published by Chengdu Municipal Government, include *Chengdu Architecture • Heritage I* as its first volume, and collect 50 historic buildings in Chengdu. They have vividly captured the existing true appearances of these historic buildings through the vicissitudes of life, recalled the century-old history and humanistic feelings carried with these historical buildings, and displayed in city development a shift from pursuing production value to life value and from economic orientation to human orientation.

In publishing this book, we have carried forward the city humanistic concept of "history and culture are the soul of a city", excavated city memories, strengthened people's overall understanding of historic buildings, expanded the breadth and depth of historic and cultural protection, promoted Chinese traditional culture, and innovatively developed the Bashu Culture, in order to let the long-standing historical accumulation support the new era concept of planning and construction in Chengdu and never fade out despite the passage of time.

成都建筑·遗珠

CHENGDU ARCHITECTURE HERITAGE

院舍祠宅

COURTYARDS, HOUSES, SHRINES AND RESIDENCES

两千三百多年来
成都城名不改城址不变
历经朝代更替战乱兵燹
以开放包容的气度、都会之城的胸襟广纳八方英贤
是以宗庙祠堂香火不绝
人才辈出绵延古今
本土与外来相融相生
东方与西方交相辉映
一座座见证着初始、记录着变革的屋宇
都是沉淀在川西大地上的精魂……

For over 2,300 years,
the name and site of the city of Chengdu has remained unchanged.
Suffering dynasty replacement, wars and turmoil,
it has accommodated persons of virtue from afar with its open inclusive capital-city mind.
Ancestral temples and shrines have been with continuous burned joss sticks and candles,
and talents have come forth generations after generations till now.
Natives and non-natives coexist and get along well with each other,
and the east and the west are complemented by each other.
Houses that have witnessed the history and recorded transformations
are all souls settling down in West Sichuan …

KANG JIHONG'S MANSION
康季鸿公馆

建筑名称：康季鸿公馆

建筑地址：锦江区通盈街 699 号

建筑面积：444.36 平方米

建筑年代：20 世纪 40 年代末至 50 年代初

Building Name: Kang Jihong's Mansion

Location: 699 Tongying Street, Jinjiang District

Built-up Area: 444.36 square meters

Completion: Late1940s to early 1950s

康季鸿公馆
一座见证了成都近现代工业文明史的中西合璧建筑

康季鸿公馆
Kang Jihong's Mansion

KANG JIHONG'S MANSION

康季鸿公馆

康季鸿公馆是民国时期成都知名企业家康季鸿的寓所，是成都近现代民族资本家私宅的唯一遗存。该公馆原有东、西两栋，东侧中式风格建筑已无存，现存西侧建筑为青砖墙壁、小青瓦坡屋顶，具有近代中西合璧的建筑特征。曾为康季鸿的食品公司办公处，1951 年收归国有后，设立过国营成都食品制造厂、成都罐头食品厂办公处，1998 年后为民营企业使用。该公馆见证了成都近现代民族私营企业改造为国有企业又演变为民营企业的全过程。

Kang Jihong's Mansion was the residence of Kang Jihong, a famous entrepreneur in Chengdu during the period of the Republic of China. It is the only preserved private residence of a national capitalist in Chengdu in modern times. Formerly, the mansion had two buildings. The east Chinese style building has disappeared. Only the west building remains. It has black-brick walls and a Chinese-style-tile pitched roof, showing modern Chinese and western integrated architectural features. It was once used as the office of Kang Jihong's food company. After it was nationalized in 1951, it was then used as the office of State-owned Chengdu Food Factory and Chengdu Canned Food Factory. After 1998, it was used by a private enterprise. This mansion witnessed the whole transformation process of private enterprises, which was transformed into state-owned enterprises first and then transformed into private enterprises again, in Chengdu in modern times.

一座见证了成都近现代工业文明史的中西合璧建筑

A Chinese-Western Building Witnessing the History of Modern Industrial Civilization in Chengdu

巫氏大夫第

巫氏大夫第 清

WU'S OFFICIAL MANSION

建筑名称：巫氏大夫第

建筑地址：龙泉驿区洛带镇下街 105 号

建筑面积：400 平方米

建筑年代：清乾隆年间

Building Name: Wu's Official Mansion

Location: 105 Xiajie Street, Luodai Town, Longquanyi District

Built-up Area: 400 square meters

Completion: During the reign of Emperor Qianlong in the Qing Dynasty

在龙泉驿区洛带镇下街，坐落着一座形制独特、造型庄重的客家民居，它由广东龙川县巫氏家族迁居四川的第二代传人巫作江所建，巫作江曾在清嘉庆时期被敕封“奉直大夫”，故该建筑名为“巫氏大夫第”。原为多重四合院落，现存一进，为木结构建筑，穿逗式梁架，悬山顶，小青瓦屋面，做工考究的各式花格木窗上雕琢着形态逼真的花鸟虫鱼，正堂保存有巫氏神案、供牌、匾额等。整个建筑可作为客家移民在四川生产、生活场景的研究样本。现属巫氏后人所有，用作民居、祠堂，兼作农家乐。

巫氏大夫第
WU'S OFFICIAL MANSION

There is a particularly-shaped solemn Hakka folk house on Xiajie Street, Luodai Town, Longquanyi District. It was built by Wu Zuojiang, the second generation of the Wu's family who migrated to Sichuan from Longchuan County in Guangdong Province. Wu Zuojiang was once appointed as a senior official (Fengzhi Dafu) during the reign of Emperor Jiaqing in the Qing Dynasty. Therefore the building was named Wu's Official Mansion. Initially, it had multiple quadrangle courtyards. Now only one courtyard remains. As a wooden building, it has pillars and transverse beams, overhanging gable roof and Chinese-style-tile roof surface. Vivid flower, bird, worm and fish patterns were carved on well-made wooden windows. Nowadays sacrificing platforms, tablets and boards are kept in the main hall. The whole building may be used as a sample for studying the Hakka's production and life in Sichuan Province. Now it is owned by a descendant of the Wu's family and used as a folk house, ancestral hall and agritainment site.

平陽世澤
四川巫氏宗親會
清正忠良
保義王家輝祖德
克臣相職煥宗功
巫氏堂上歷代先
前言
溯源寻根
中国历史与巫氏始祖

堂屋正面墙上挂着“平阳世泽”的牌匾，贴着巫氏先祖的画像，桌上供奉着“巫氏历代先祖之神位”的牌位。

On the front wall of the main room hangs a tablet with Chinese characters of “平阳世泽” (the ancestors' graces are long-lasting), pasted with portraits of the Wu's ancestors. On the table is a memorial tablet with Chinese characters “巫氏历代先祖之神位” (a memorial talet for commemorating Wu's ancestors).

董寿平旧居

FORMER RESIDENCE OF DONG SHOUPING

建筑名称：董寿平旧居

建筑地址：都江堰市西街 122、124 号

建筑面积：62.17 平方米

建筑年代：清末民初

Building Name: Former Residence of Dong Shouping

Location: 122 and 124 West Street, Dujiangyan City

Built-up Area: 62.17 square meters

Completion: In the late Qing Dynasty and the early Republic of China

该建筑是当代著名画家、书法家董寿平(1904—1997年)先生客居都江堰时的居所。现存临街商铺两间，后院天井及住房一间，典型前店后宅模式，川西民居风格。董寿平先生在此工作生活期间，曾创作出了千余幅以青城山为背景题材的画作，并在此与文化名人张大千、林山腴、谢无量、沈尹默、徐悲鸿、赵少昂、赵望云等交往甚密。该处是研究抗战期间文人入川生活的样本。现为都江堰兴堰投资有限公司所有，由四川巴蜀书画院、四川东方张大千研究中心使用。

This building is the residence of Dong Shouping (1904-1997) – a well-known contemporary painter and calligrapher when he stayed in Dujiangyan City. What survives till now include two street shop rooms, a backyard and a bedroom. It is a typical mode of shop in the front and bedroom at the back, with a folk house style of West Sichuan. During his work and life here, Mr. Dong Shouping created some one thousand Mt. Qingcheng-themed paintings, and had close contact with famous intellectuals such as Zhang Daqian (Chang Dai-chien), Lin Shanyu, Xie Wuliang, Shen Yinmo, Xu Beihong, Zhao Shaoang, and Zhao Wangyun. It is a sample for studying the life of intellectuals in Sichuan during the Resistance against Japanese Aggression. It is now owned by Dujiangyan Xingyan Investment Co., Ltd, and used by Sichuan Bashu Painting and Calligraphy Institute and Sichuan Oriental Chang Dai-chien Research Center.

落霞與孤鶩齊
秋水共長天

欣廬
BREGUET

欣庐

XINLU BUILDING

建筑名称：欣庐

建筑地址：锦江区大慈寺街区

建筑面积：625 平方米

建筑年代：民国时期

Building Name: Xinlu Building

Location: Dacisi Block, Jinjiang District

Built-up Area: 625 square meters

Completion: During the Republic of China

欣庐

XINLU BUILDING

欣庐是大慈寺街区六处建筑遗存之一，为近代建筑风格的前店后宅式三合院，靠西糠市街为两层中式建筑。因中华人民共和国成立前最后一位主人名叫蒲欣芦而得名。该建筑吸收了中国古代建筑和民国时期建筑的精华，是近代川西城镇住宅的代表之一。整个院落以青灰色为主调，庄重典雅，朴素静谧。曾于2008年完成修复，现保存完好。

As one of the six heritage buildings in the Dacisi Block, Xinlu Building is a three-section compound with a modern architectural style, shops in the front and residence at the back. There is a two-storey Chinese-style building by Kangshi Street West. It is named after Pu Xinlu – its last owner before the founding of the People's Republic of China. The building absorbs the essence of ancient Chinese architecture and that of the architecture during the Republic of China, and it is one of the representatives of modern western Sichuan urban housing. The entire courtyard is dominated by blue-gray, appearing solemn, elegant, simple, and tranquil. Upon completion of repair in 2008, it is now well preserved.

马家巷老宅院

OLD COURTYARD HOUSE ON MAJIA ALLEY

建筑名称：马家巷老宅院

建筑地址：锦江区大慈寺街区

建筑面积：375 平方米

建筑年代：清末民初

Building Name: Old Courtyard House on Majia Alley

Location: Dacisi Block, Jinjiang District

Built-up Area: 375 square meters

Completion: In the late Qing Dynasty and the early Republic of China

玉成街 Yucheng Street
东顺城南街 Dongshuncheng Street South
和尚街 Heshang Street

建筑所在地因马姓人家聚居，形成街坊，故名马家巷。该建筑原为前来大慈寺朝拜的居士住所，是马家巷唯一现存的老建筑。建筑外观构筑精致，结构独特，呈三合院布局，耳房和堂屋均为两层。该建筑是大慈寺街区内保存较完整的传统院落。现为太古里商圈内展览、文化交流场所。

The place where the old house is located is named Majia Alley because the Ma's family lives there. Formerly, the Old House was used as a residence for Buddhists who came to the Daci Temple for worship. It is the only old building existing on Majia Alley. With a delicate appearance and particular structure, the house has a three-section compound layout. Both its side rooms and central room have two storeys. As a well-preserved traditional courtyard in the Dacisi Block, the house is now used for exhibition and cultural exchange in the Taikoo Li business district.

成都市历史建筑
HERITAGE ARCHITECTURE
马家巷禅院

章华里老宅院

ZHANGHUALI OLD COURTYARD HOUSE

建筑名称：章华里老宅院
建筑地址：锦江区大慈寺街区
建筑面积：525 平方米
建筑年代：民国初年

Building Name: Zhanghuali Old Courtyard House
Location: Dacisi Block, Jinjiang District
Built-up Area: 525 square meters
Completion: In the early Republic of China

章华里，原为大慈寺东禅堂的桑园，1925年修建住房后形成里弄，为称颂主人文章才华，故名“章华里”。该宅院为章华里仅存的建筑，带有浓郁的川西民居特色，布局独特，对于保留“里”这一老成都街道符号具有重要作用，并与大慈寺街区内的其他老建筑构成了一个历史建筑群落，保留并传承了老成都的街道传统文化。

Zhanghuali used to be a mulberry field in the east meditation room of the Daci Temple. After residential houses were built in 1925, a neighborhood came into being. In order to praise the owner's excellent writing skill, it was named Zhanghuali. This old courtyard house is the only survived building at Zhanghuali. Since it is full of characteristics of western Sichuan folk houses and has a particular layout, it plays an important role in retaining the street name "li" (meaning "lane"), an old street symbol in Chengdu. This building and other old buildings in the Dacisi Block make up a community of historical buildings, retaining and carrying on the traditional street culture of Old Chengdu.

笔帖式街老宅院

OLD COURTYARD HOUSE ON BITIESHI STREET

建筑名称：笔帖式街老宅院

建筑地址：大慈寺街区内

建筑面积：1220 平方米

建筑年代：清末民初

Building Name: Old Courtyard House on Bitieshi Street

Location: In the Dacisi Block

Built-up Area: 1,220 square meters

Completion: In the late Qing Dynasty and the early Republic of China

笔帖式街老宅院 清

OLD COURTYARD HOUSE ON BITIESHI STREET

建于清代晚期，原为清代笔帖式署衙门所在地，后改为住居宅院。“笔帖式”是满语的音译汉写，是清代总督府之下专门设立的一种负责掌管满文与汉文翻译事务的官职，笔帖式办公的地方叫“笔帖式署”，笔帖式街因此得名，它是成都市唯一一条以满语译音为街名的街道。该建筑系笔帖式街仅存的老宅院，是一处典型的川西民居建筑风格的四合院，也是清代成都历史的重要见证。

Built in the late Qing Dynasty, it used to be the governmental agency of Bitieshi Office in the Qing Dynasty, later used as a residential house with a courtyard. Bitieshi is a transliteration from the Manchu language, which is an official title for translators between the Manchu language and the Chinese language under the Governor's Office in the Qing Dynasty. Bitieshi Office was the place where they worked, hence the name Bitieshi Street, which is the only street named after a transliteration from the Manchu language. This building is the only survival old courtyard house on Bitieshi Street, and it is a typical quadrangle courtyard house with folk architecture style of West Sichuan and a vital witness to the history of Chengdu in the Qing Dynasty.

唐昌镇杨公馆

YANG'S MANSION IN TANGCHANG TOWN

建筑名称：唐昌镇杨公馆
建筑地址：郫县唐昌镇文山路93号
唐昌幼儿园内
建筑面积：590平方米
建筑年代：清光绪年间

Building Name: Yang's Mansion in Tangchang Town
Location: In Tangchang Kindergarten, 93 Wenshan Road, Tangchang Town, Pixian County
Built-up Area: 590 square meters
Completion: During the reign of Emperor Guangxu in the Qing Dynasty

唐昌镇杨公馆

YANG'S MANSION IN TANGCHANG TOWN

该建筑始建于清光绪年间，占地面积 1515 平方米，原系某酱园主所有，后为杨汇川所有，经其子杨继麟、其孙杨世煊两代人改建为唐昌镇风貌独特的公馆。1950 年后，杨公馆改建为唐昌幼儿园，现由幼儿园作为教室使用。该建筑为木结构，体量较大，结构精巧，是唐昌镇保留完整、富有特色的传统建筑之一，对于了解民国时期唐昌镇的城市风貌、人居文化和民居特征，具有重要的价值和意义。

Covering a land area of 1,515 square meters, this building was first built during the reign of Emperor Guangxu in the Qing Dynasty. Initially it was owned by a sauce and pickle shop owner. After it was owned by Yang Huichuan, it was rebuilt by his son, Yang Jilin, and his grandson, Yang Shixuan, being a particularly-shaped mansion in Tangchang Town. In 1950, Yang's Mansion was rebuilt into Tangchang Kindergarten. Now it is used as a classroom. With an exquisite timber structure, this building is very large. It is one of well-conserved characteristic traditional buildings in Tangchang Town. It is of great value and significance for learning about Tangchang Town's cityscape, dwelling culture and folk residence feature during the period of the Republic of China.

张大千故居掩映在一片绿树之中。20 世纪 40 年代，离开成都之前，张大千就在这里居住。

Former Residence of Zhang Daqian sits amid green woods, and it is the place where Zhang Daqian stayed in the 1940s before he left Chengdu.

民國

张大千故居

FORMER RESIDENCE OF ZHANG DAQIAN

建筑名称：张大千故居

建筑地址：金牛区金泉路 2 号金牛宾馆内

建筑面积：324 平方米

建筑年代：20 世纪 40 年代

Building Name: Former Residence of Zhang Daqian

Location: In Jinniu Hotel, 2 Jinquan Road, Jinniu District

Built-up Area: 324 square meters

Completion: In the 1940s

民国时期张大千往来成都时的寓所，后辟为“大千茶居”。砖木结构，青砖青瓦，整套建筑的构建手法较为简练，大门、柱头、栏杆、房檐都仅以简单的线条作修饰。张大千是 20 世纪中国画坛顶级国画大师，被西方艺坛赞为“东方之笔”，作为大千先生在成都的居所，张大千故居具有非常重要的纪念意义和丰富的人文内涵。

This building was Zhang Daqian (Chang Dai-chien)'s residence when he stayed in Chengdu during the period of the Republic of China. Later it was rebuilt into a teahouse, named Daqian Teahouse. With a brick-timber structure, it was made of black bricks and Chinese style tiles. The whole building was built in a concise way. Entrance, chapiter, guardrail and eaves were decorated only with simple lines. Zhang Daqian was a top traditional Chinese painting master in China in the 20th century. He was regarded as the "Oriental Pen" by Western art circles. As Zhang Daqian's residence in Chengdu, this building has a significant memorial meaning and abundant cultural connotations.

好日子舒心顺意

苏继贤
旧居

FORMER RESIDENCE OF WALTER SMALL

建筑名称：苏继贤旧居

建筑地址：武侯区人民南路 17 号四川大学华西校区内

建筑面积：767 平方米

建筑年代：20 世纪 20 年代

Building Name: Former Residence of Walter Small

Location: In Sichuan University Huaxi Campus, 17 Renmin Road South, Wuhou District

Built-up Area: 767 square meters

Completion: In the 1920s

大学路 University Road

人民南路 Renmin Road South

胜利村 Shengli Village

林荫街 Linyin Street

该建筑为华西协合大学加拿大籍建筑工程师苏继贤（Walter Small）定居成都时设计建造并自住的住宅。苏继贤擅长使用木质建筑材料，人称“苏木匠”，曾主持修建了华西医科大学图书馆、钟楼、牙科大楼、化学楼等诸多重要建筑。旧居外观上糅合了贵格建筑造型风格与川西民居特色，两层砖木结构，保存完好，画栋飞檐，青砖灰瓦，掩映林中；屋内壁炉烟囱一应俱全，中西合璧、极富特色。20世纪五六十年代多位专家教授曾居住于此，后被用作教职工宿舍。它与华西坝其他老建筑共同展现着东西方文化在成都的碰撞与交融。

This building was designed and built by Walter Small, a Canadian architectural engineer of West China Union University, and used as his residence when he lived in Chengdu. Because Walter Small is good at using wooden building materials, he is called "Carpenter Walter Small" by people. He once took charge of construction of many important buildings, including library of West China University of Medical Sciences, bell tower, Dental Building and Chemistry Building, etc. The residence shows a Quaker architectural style and feature of western Sichuan folk house. With a brick-timber structure, it has two floors. The building is well conserved, with painted eaves, black bricks and Chinese style tiles. It is equipped with a fireplace and chimney, showing typical Chinese and Western architectural characteristics. In the 1950s and the 1960s, many experts and professors once lived in this building. Later it was used as a dorm for faculties. It displays the clash and integration of Eastern and Western cultures in Chengdu along with other old buildings at Huaxiba.

绣花楼

贺麟故居

FORMER RESIDENCE OF HE LIN

建筑名称：贺麟故居

建筑地址：金堂县五凤镇金箱村 2 组

建筑面积：约 3200 平方米

建筑年代：清乾隆八年（1743 年）

Building Name: Former Residence of He Lin

Location: Group 2, Jinxiang Village, Wufeng Town, Jintang County

Built-up Area: Approximately 3,200 square meters

Completion: In the the 8th year during the reign of Emperor Qianlong in the Qing Dynasty (1743)

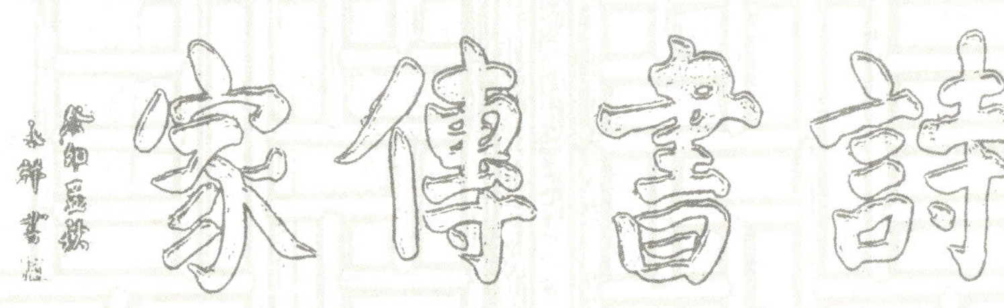
詩書傳家

该建筑由贺麟太祖父贺才榜修建，建筑占地面积10.86亩。中国当代著名西方哲学史家、翻译家和教育家贺麟在此诞生，并度过了青少年时光。

故居前临杨柳河，背倚寨子山，竹林掩映，为青瓦灰砖土木结构二进四合院，有房八十余间。该建筑选址考究，布局严谨，功能齐全，建筑手法独特，部件、装饰精美，是典型的清代乡绅私宅。现为贺麟故居纪念馆馆舍，设有贺麟与民盟陈列室、先哲堂、贺麟生平事迹陈列馆、贺蕴章生平事迹陈列室、祠堂等，陈列有贺氏家族文物和贺麟先生手稿、书籍、物品。

This building was built by He Lin's great grandfather – He Caibang, covering a land of 10.86 mu (some 7,000 square meters). He Lin, a noted contemporary Western philosophy historian, translator and educator of China, was born and spent his youth time here.

Amid a bamboo forest, this former residence is adjacent to the Yangliu River in its front, and backs on the Zhaizi Mountain. It is a two-tier quadrangle courtyard house, with Chinese style tiles, gray bricks and in an earth and wood structure, composed of more than 80 rooms. The site of this building was carefully selected, with a conscientious layout and complete functions. The architectural manners are unique, and components and decorations are exquisite, so it is a typical private house of country gentlemen in the Qing Dynasty. It is now the Former Residence Memorial of He Lin, including the Exhibition Room of He Lin and China Democratic League, the Hall of Sages, the Exhibition Room of He Lin's Deeds and Achievements, the Exhibition Room of He Yunzhang's Deeds and Achievements, and the Ancestral Shrine, with cultural relics of the He's family and Mr. He Lin's manuscripts, books and items.

贺麟故居大朝门，上有著名书法家、国家一级美术师张幼矩先生题匾篆书“心园”。

On the front gate of the Former Residence of He Lin, there hangs an inscribed tablet with two Chinese seal characters “心园” (Heart Garden), written by Mr. Zhang Youju – a famous calligrapher and national first-class artist.

李育滋公馆

民國

LI YUZI'S MANSION

建筑名称：李育滋公馆
建筑地址：大邑县安仁镇新团村2组
建筑面积：940.56 平方米
建筑年代：1940 年

Building Name: Li Yuzi's Mansion
Location: Group 2, Xintuan Village, Anren Town, Dayi County
Built-up Area: 940.56 square meters
Completion: In 1940

成温邛快速路 Chengdu-Wenjiang-Qionglai Freeway
街安路 Jie'an Street
大新路 Daxin Road

该建筑为民国时期安仁镇士绅李育滋的公馆。公馆占地面积3916平方米，为不规则多边形封闭式院落，共有六进院落和一个花园。建筑以砖木结构为主，小青瓦屋面，内宅院地面用方砖铺筑。建筑屋顶形式采用单檐悬山式、歇山式和硬山式，木构件撑弓、天官罩均装饰了传统的吉祥图案。该建筑体量较大，装饰精美，具有鲜明的时代特征和较高的建筑价值。

This building was the residence of Li Yuzi, a rich businessman in Anren Town during the period of the Republic of China. Covering a land area of 3,916 square meters, it is an irregular polygonal closed courtyard house, with six tiers and one garden. Most of the buildings have a brick-timber structure and Chinese-style-tile roof. The floor of the internal courtyard is paved with square bricks. Different rooms have different roof forms, including single-eaves overhanging gable roof, gable and hip roof, and flush gable roof. Strut bows and covers of timber structures etc. are all decorated with traditional auspicious patterns. The mansion is very large and well decorated, with vivid characteristics of the times as well as a high architectural value.

大门具有中西合璧的风格。

The entrance reflects a Chinese and Western integrated style.

古城镇古井院

ANCIENT WELL COURTYARD IN GUCHENG TOWN

建筑名称：古城镇古井院

建筑地址：郫都区古城镇蜀汉中街 36 号

建筑面积：240 平方米

建筑年代：清同治年间

Building Name: Ancient Well Courtyard in Gucheng Town

Location: 36 Middle Shuhan Street, Gucheng Town, Pidu District

Built-up Area: 240 square meters

Completion: During the reign of Emperor Tongzhi of the Qing Dynasty

福

建于清同治年间，距今已有 140 多年的历史，全木质结构，是川西民居风格的四合院。院内天井有一银盘古井，相传由三国时期留下，古井四季不枯，水质纯洁清甜，故名古井院。该建筑最初修建者为杨氏先祖，至今已传承六代，现为杨孟明及丈夫马贤寿所有。该建筑是古城街道内目前仅存的清代时期木结构建筑，杨氏后人世代居住其间，具备较好的历史原真性与完整性，对了解清代时期古城街道的城镇风貌、人居文化和民居特征，具有重要的价值和意义。

It was built during the reign of Emperor Tongzhi of the Qing Dynasty, with a history of more than 140 years. In a fully wooden structure, it is a quadrangle courtyard house with a folk house style of West Sichuan. There is a silver-plated ancient well in the courtyard. It is said that the well was left from the Three Kingdoms period, which contains water throughout the year, pure and sweet, hence the name Ancient Well Courtyard. The building was originally built by the Yang's ancestors and has been inherited for six generations. It is now owned by Yang Mengming and her husband Ma Xianshou. This building is the only remaining wooden structure from the Qing Dynasty in Gucheng Sub-district, and the descendants of the Yang's family have lived for generations. With good historical authenticity and integrity, this courtyard is of important value and significance to understanding the urban style, human settlement culture, and folk house characteristics in Gucheng Sub-district during the Qing Dynasty.

古城镇古井院

ANCIENT WELL COURTYARD IN GUCHENG TOWN

启庐 民國

QI LU BUILDING

建筑名称：启庐

建筑地址：锦江区新开街 84 号

建筑面积：580 平方米

建筑年代：民国时期（1930—1940 年）

Building Name: Qi Lu Building

Location: 84 Xinkai Street, Jinjiang District

Built-up Area: 580 square meters

Completion: During the Republic of China (1930-1940)

该建筑是民国时期典型的公馆建筑，原为砖木结构，工艺精细，屋面线条流畅，撑弓、花罩等木构件雕刻精美，修缮后保持了原有的风貌和精美的砖门斗。建筑由正房和两侧厢房围合，呈三合院布局，正房南侧设有地下室，门斗布置在北厢房北侧，外形简洁大方，建筑体量、工艺均高于普通民宅，具有成都地区民国公馆建筑的特征。

This building is a typical mansion in the period of the Republic of China. Originally it has a brick-timber structure. It was built with exquisite craftsmanship. On the roof are smooth lines and some wood structures, such as strut bows and carved covers. After repair, its original appearance and the exquisite brick door bucket have remained. The building is encircled by the principal room and wing rooms at both sides, showing a three-section compound layout. In the south of the principal room is a basement. The door bucket is located in the north of the north wing room, looking simple and elegant. This building is superior to ordinary residential houses in terms of architectural volume and craftsmanship, with characteristics of mansions in Chengdu during the period of the Republic of China.

友爱镇
徐家大院老宅

XU'S OLD COURTYARD HOUSE IN YOUAI TOWN

建筑名称：友爱镇徐家大院老宅

建筑地址：郫都区友爱镇徐家大院乡村酒店内

建筑面积：304.6 平方米

建筑年代：20 世纪 80 年代初

Building Name: Xu's Old Courtyard House in Youai Town

Location: In Xu's Courtyard Rural Hotel, Youai Town, Pidu District

Built-up Area: 304.6 square meters

Completion: In the early 1980s

源居
Suyuan house
第一代农家乐原址
老树老院柴门初开迎貴客

徐家大院是改革开放后中国最早兴起的农家乐之一，30 余年间，从最初的一栋红砖青瓦房发展到现在的酒店式四星级农家乐，为三代农家乐同院。本画册中的建筑为第一代农家乐原址，占地面积 731 平方米，建于 1985 年，1987 年翻修，具有川西民居的特点。它与 20 世纪 90 年代第二代农家乐的原址——一栋两层蓝色别墅，以及今天的第三代农家乐建筑群，一起见证了中国农家乐起源及发展的活态历程，是新农村乡村旅游的典范。由此，2006 年成都被中国国家旅游局授予"中国农家乐发源地"称号，在农业创新发展中起到了示范作用。

Xu's Courtyard is one of the earliest courtyards used for agritainment in China after China started its reform and opening-up policy. Through more than 30 years' development, it has grown into a hotel-style four-star agritainment business, i.e. a 3-generation agritainment courtyard. The building in this picture album is the original site of Generation-I agritainment, covering a land area of 731 square meters. It was built in 1985 and renovated in 1987, with features of western Sichuan folk houses. It witnessed the start and development process of agritainment in China along with Generation-II agritainment (a two-storey blue villa) built in the 1990s and today's Generation-III agritainment building complex, being a role model of new rural travel. For this reason, Chengdu was named the "cradle of agritourism in China" by China National Tourism Administration in 2006 and it played an exemplary role in the process of innovative agricultural development.

友爱镇
徐家大院老宅

XU'S OLD COURTYARD HOUSE IN YOUAI TOWN

广兴镇
刁氏宗祠

DIAO’S ANCESTRAL SHRINE IN GUANGXING TOWN

建筑名称：广兴镇刁氏宗祠
建筑地址：金堂县广兴镇广严寺社区三组
建筑面积：392 平方米
建筑年代：清代

Building Name: Diao’s Ancestral Shrine in Guangxing Town
Location: Group 3, Guangyansi Community, Guangxing Town, Jintang County
Built-up Area: 392 square meters
Completion: In the Qing Dynasty

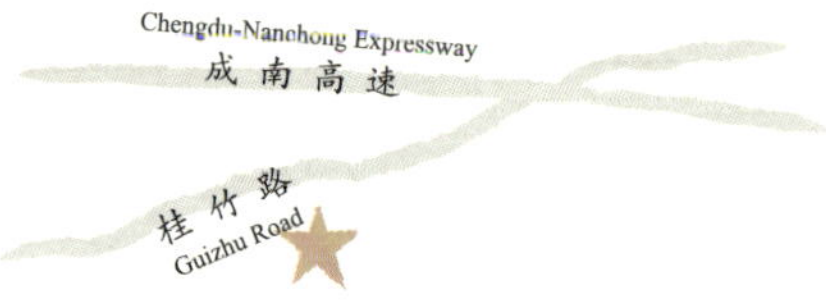

建筑素面台基高 5.4 米，垂带踏道 19 级，循阶而上的主殿为供奉刁氏历代祖先之场所。

The undecorated platform base of this building is 5.4m high; there are 19 steps with drooping belt stones; the main hall up the steps is the site for worshipping the Diao’s ancestors of all ages.

建筑面阔5间12米，进深2间6米，通高5.5米，明间采用木抬梁式屋架，次稍间为穿逗式屋架。

The building width extends for 5 rooms, 12 meters; its depth is 2 rooms, 6 meters; the full height is 5.5 meters. The external rooms are with roof trusses of wooden post and lintel construction, and the side rooms are with roof trusses of column and tie construction.

清乾隆七年（1742年）刁家始祖刁荣桂携妻偕子由广东入川，定居广兴镇。后人在此修建宗祠，以纪念先祖，亦作为族人聚会之地。祠堂选址考究，背山面水，坐北向南，呈“凸字形”，采用四合院布局，建筑规模宏大，规制完整，雕刻构件精美，为典型的客家祠堂建筑。建筑为石木结构，采用巨大圆木作支撑柱，以木板、石板为墙壁，庄重古朴。祠堂至今保存完整，记载有大量家训、家规，为研究当地清代的家族文化和建筑特征提供了重要的实物例证。

In the 7th year of Emperor Qianlong of the Qing Dynasty (1742), the ancestor of the Diao's family – Diao Ronggui, emigrated with his wife and son from Guangdong and settled down in Guangxing Town, Sichuan Province. Later generations built the ancestral shrine to commemorate the ancestors, which has also served as a gathering place for the Diao's families. The site of the ancestral shrine was carefully selected, with the mountain at the back and water in front, sitting in the north and facing the south, and in a "convex" layout. In the structure of a quadrangle courtyard house, it has a magnificent building scale, complete shapes, and exquisite carving components. It is a typical Hakka-style ancestral shrine. The building is made of stones and wood, with huge round logs as supporting columns and wooden boards and slates as walls, solemn and primitive. This ancestral shrine has been well preserved to this day, and there are a large quantity of records on family injunctions and family rules, providing essential real-object examples for studying the family culture and architectural features of the Qing Dynasty.

建筑采用石质柱础，木质梁柱，梁柱间使用撑弓、吊瓜构件装饰，窗格雕刻有精美花鸟图样。

The building adopts a stone column foundation and wooden beams and columns, and strut bows and hanging components are applied between beams and columns for decoration; the panes are engraved with beautiful flowers and birds.

兴义镇
刘家院子

LIU'S COURTYARD IN XINGYI TOWN

建筑名称：兴义镇刘家院子
建筑地址：新津县兴义镇岷江社区菜棚子林盘内
建筑面积：145 平方米
建筑年代：20 世纪 50 年代初

Building Name: Liu's Courtyard in Xingyi Town
Location: In the Caipengzi Farmhouse Forest, Minjiang Community, Xingyi Town, Xinjin County
Built-up Area: 145 square meters
Completion: In the early 1950s

该建筑所在的岷江菜棚子是原汁原味的川西林盘，林盘中水清林密，刘家院子掩映其中，用围墙隔成独立的院落，房前屋后遍种竹木，如同一派水墨画。刘家院子建于中华人民共和国成立初期，后于2009年改建，占地面积450平方米，砖木结构，有房屋7间，框架均用木头搭就，墙体用黄泥垒砌，窗户也是全木质，未安装玻璃，完全保留了川西传统民居的风格。该建筑为了解川西地区乡村房屋建筑形制提供了实物资料，对研究传统的农耕文化具有重要意义。原属我国杰出人民教育家刘绍禹家族所有，现归兴义镇政府所有，用于参观展览。

Caipengzi Farmhouse Forest, where this building is located, is an original western Sichuan farmhouse forest. Liu's Courtyard is located right in a dense forest with clear water. The independent courtyard is surrounded by fences. Bamboos and trees are planted around the house, constituting a wash painting. Liu's Courtyard was built soon after the founding of the People's Republic of China. In 2009, it was rebuilt. Covering a land area of 450 square meters, the brick-timber-structure courtyard has 7 rooms, with wood windows but no glass, and walls were built with yellow soils, retaining the traditional western Sichuan folk house style. This building may be used to learn about the structure of rural houses in western Sichuan and it is of great significance to the research of traditional farming culture. Initially the building was owned by Liu Shaoyu, an outstanding Chinese educator. Now it is owned by the government of Xingyi Town and used for sightseeing and exhibition.

兴义镇 刘家院子

LIU'S COURTYARD IN XINGYI TOWN

廖启清故居

民國

FORMER RESIDENCE OF LIAO QIQING

建筑名称：廖启清故居

建筑地址：蒲江县寿安镇插旗山村6组

建筑面积：120平方米

建筑年代：民国

Building Name: Former Residence of Liao Qiqing

Location: Group 6, Chaqishan Village, Shouan Town, Pujiang County

Built-up Area: 120 square meters

Completion: During the Republic of China

该建筑院内设有通风天井，形成良好的"穿堂风"，檐廊或柱廊联系着各个房间，灵巧组成街坊。

There is a ventilating light court in the courtyard, producing excellent draught. The eaves gallery or colonnade links all rooms together, delicately forming a housing block.

该建筑为当地文化名人廖启清的故居，建于民国时期，木穿逗结构，黄土为坯，草木为梭，以木为梁，以竹为屏，溯往可追百余年。传统川西庭院式民居，布局风格开敞自山，山 ·正两厢 下房组成的“四合头”房。建筑造型风格轻盈精巧，斜坡顶、薄封檐，开敞通透。建筑梁柱断面较小，外墙体采用高勒脚、半桩台，室内用木地板架空。建筑色彩朴素淡雅，建筑四周植被较好，四季常青。入口门楼，俗称“龙门”，“雕而不画”，质朴淡雅。

This building was once the residence of Liao Qiqing, a well-known cultural celebrity. Built during the period of the Republic of China, this residence has a timber column and tie construction. Its walls are made of yellow soil, ridges made of grass and timber, girders made of timber, and barriers made of bamboos. With a history of more than 100 years, the building is a traditional western Sichuan courtyard residence with an open layout. It has one main room, two wing rooms, and one servant room, in a square arrangement. With a light and delicate architectural modeling style, it has inclined pitched roofs and thin eaves. It is open and bright. Its beams and columns have small sections. Exterior walls have high plinths and half-pile platforms. Its interior is paved with elevated timber flooring. The architectural color is simple and elegant. The building is encircled by plants, which are green throughout the year. At the entrance of the building is a gate tower (also known as the Dragon Gate), with simple and unadorned carvings.

廖启清故居 民國

FORMER RESIDENCE OF LIAO QIQING

院落中的天井与宽屋檐、住宅外的檐廊，为居住者创造了一个较明朗的生活、工作的“公用空间”，供家人纳凉、妇女手工、小孩嬉戏、邻里喝茶下棋以及接待来客之用，体现了蜀人的人情味、亲情味。

The ventilating light court and wide eaves in the courtyard and the eaves gallery outside the residence provide a bright "public space" to dwellers, where they can enjoy cold wind, do handwork, play for fun, drink tea, play chess or receive visitors. This building reflects Sichuan people's attention to humanity and affection among family members.

贺家大院 清

HE'S GRAND COURTYARD

建筑名称：贺家大院

建筑地址：金堂县五凤镇金箱村

建筑面积：约 500 平方米

建筑年代：清嘉庆十四年（1809 年）

Building Name: He's Grand Courtyard

Location: Jinxiang Village, Wufeng Town, Jintang County

Built-up Area: Approximately 500 square meters

Completion: In the 14th year during the reign of Emperor Jiaqing in the Qing Dynasty (1809)

大院前厅采用悬山式屋顶，抬梁式梁架。

The front hall of the courtyard is with overhanging gable roofs and a post and lintel construction.

贺家大院由湖南移民贺奇瑜修建，占地面积约1000平方米。该建筑为川西民居建筑风格，由前厅、正堂及左右厢房组成，土木结构，青瓦屋面，呈四合院布局。院内正堂保存较好，尚存“锄经”等匾额6块，楹联3副，对研究清代移民文化、清代中后期当地民居建筑形制、风格及贺氏家族史具有重要意义。现为民居，改造后将用于研究、教育、参观学习以及人文旅游、休闲娱乐场所。

He's Grand Courtyard was built by He Qiyu – an emigrant from Hunan, covering an area of approximately 1,000 square meters. This building is with a folk house style of West Sichuan, composed of the front hall, the main hall and left and right wing rooms. It is of an earth and wood structure, with a Chinese-style-tile roof and in a layout of quadrangle courtyard. The main hall in the courtyard is well preserved, and there still remain 6 inscribed tablets such as "Chu Jing" (hoe scripture) and 3 couplets on pillars, which are of vital significance to studying the emigrant culture in the Qing Dynasty, the local folk house architecture and style in the middle and late periods of the Qing Dynasty, and the history of the He's family. It is now a folk house, and is planned to serve purposes of research, education, visit, learning, cultural tourism, leisure and entertainment after renovation.

善為作善為承一代宏謨繩祖武

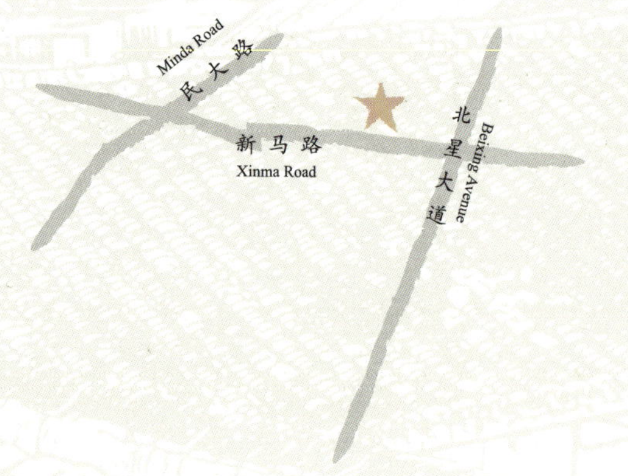

刘氏宗祠 清

LIU'S ANCESTRAL SHRINE

建筑名称：刘氏宗祠

建筑地址：新都区斑竹园镇三河村5组

建筑面积：600平方米

建筑年代：清康熙五十八年（1719年）

Building Name: Liu's Ancestral Shrine

Location: Group 5, Sanhe Village, Banzhuyuan Town, Xindu District

Built-up Area: 600 square meters

Completion: In the 58th year during the reign of Emperor Kangxi in the Qing Dynasty (1719)

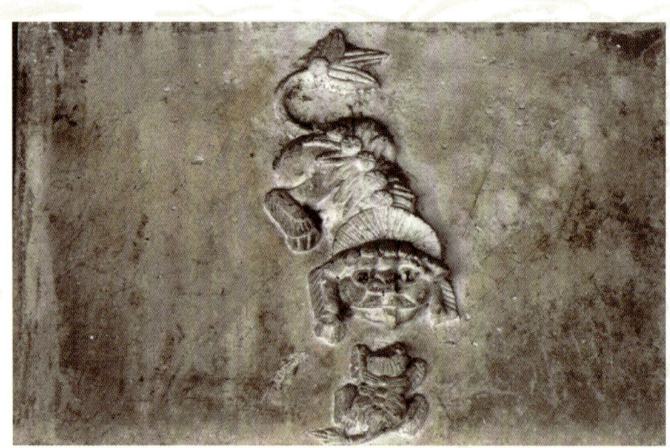

据民国十三年（1924年）《刘氏族谱》记载，刘氏宗祠为广东梅州兴宁水口镇移民刘中和所建。刘氏始祖刘开七在南宋嘉定年间官授潮州都统制，镇守粤东，保境息民，后因平定叛乱为国捐躯。祠堂呈四合院布局，采用木穿逗结构，竹笆泥壁，青瓦坡式的屋顶，解决了多雨季节的屋面排水难题。建筑外墙以白色为基础色调，利于反光，弥补了采光不足的缺陷。枣红廊柱、浅褐门窗，搭配白墙愈显清新淡雅，蕴藏川西民居婉约气质。现属刘氏家族所有，主要用作祠堂祭祀，对于研究客家人在四川的生产、生活及刘氏家族历史具有重要价值。

According to the *Pedigree of Liu's Clan* made in the 13th year of the period of the Republic of China (1924), Liu's Ancestral Shrine was built by Liu Zhonghe, an emigrant from Shuikou Town, Xingning, Meizhou, Guangdong Province. His ancestor, Liu Kaiqi, was the commander of Chaozhou during the Jiading period of the Southern Song Dynasty, responsible for guarding east Guangdong Province. Later Liu Kaiqi died for the country when putting down a rebellion. The Ancestral Shrine has a quadrangle courtyard layout, timber column and tie construction, bamboo fence, mud wall, and Chinese-style-tile pitched roof. Rain can flow down easily in rainy seasons. Its white exterior wall is good for reflecting light, making up for the deficiency of daylight. In addition, the Ancestral Shrine has purplish red columns and light brown windows and doors. Thus it looks refreshing, simple and elegant, showing western Sichuan residence's graceful and restrained manner. Now the Ancestral Shrine is owned by the Liu's family, used for sacrificial ceremonies. It is of important value for making a study of Hakka's production and life in Sichuan Province as well as the Liu's clan history.

刘氏宗祠

LIU'S ANCESTRAL SHRINE

十二中街 4 号民居

FOLK HOUSE AT 4 SHIER ZHONGJIE STREET

立面以清水砖墙为主同时兼有拉毛抹灰面与水泥砂浆面。

Its facade is an undecorated brick wall with a blurred plastering surface and cement mortar surface.

建筑名称：十二中街4号民居

建筑地址：武侯区十二中街4号

建筑面积：96.8平方米

建筑年代：1938年

Building Name: Folk House at 4 Shier Zhongjie Street

Location: 4 Shier Zhongjie Street, Wuhou District

Built-up Area: 96.8 square meters

Completion: In 1938

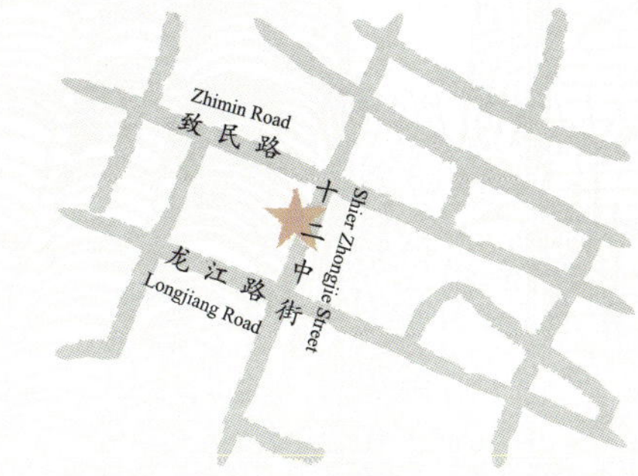

民国时期为一私人住宅。整个建筑呈简欧风格，砖木结构，造型简洁得体，色彩朴实素雅，没有多余装饰，但又不失空间虚实变化。建造充分考虑到川西地区多雨少风的气候特点，采用了本地特色的小青瓦坡屋顶。1949年后由市民政局接管，供师级老红军王桂斌、唐桂蓉夫妇居住。现属市民政局所有，作为一家特色餐吧，延续着其质朴又极具实用价值的建筑生命。

This folk house was a private residence during the period of the Republic of China. With a simple European style, the whole building has a brick-timber structure. It looks simple but decent, with plain colors and spatial changes but no redundant decoration. The climatic feature of “much rain and little wind” in western Sichuan was fully taken into consideration as this house was built. Therefore, locally-characteristic Chinese-style-tile pitched roof was used. In 1949, this house was taken over by the Municipal Civil Affairs Bureau and supplied to a division-level Red Army couple, Wang Guibin and Tang Guirong, as residence. Now it is owned by the Municipal Civil Affairs Bureau and used as a characteristic restaurant to extend its life that is simple but of practical value.

徐子昌旧居

FORMER RESIDENCE OF XU ZICHANG

建筑名称：徐子昌旧居
建筑地址：金牛区花牌坊街 2 号成都工业学校内
建筑面积：303.6 平方米
建筑年代：20 世纪 30 年代中期

Building Name: Former Residence of Xu Zichang
Location: In Chengdu Technological University, 2 Huapaifang Street, Jinniu District
Built-up Area: 303.6 square meters
Completion: In the middle 1930s

中华人民共和国成立前成都警务司令部督查主任徐子昌的住宅。该建筑立面三段式构图鲜明建筑各部位比例适当，具有典型的中西合璧风格特征。其基座台阶为川西特产红砂石砌体，墙体与檐柱采用青砖错花精砌，正面檐柱为原型希腊柱式，后面为磨砖倒角方柱，砌筑工艺精美。建筑为歇山坡屋顶，小青瓦屋面，左右山墙有歇山顶门廊，将西方和成都地方建筑风格融合较好，协调自然，是成都市内保存较好的近现代公馆建筑的代表。现为四川当代油画院办公场所。

This building was the residence of Xu Zichang, supervision director of Chengdu Police Affairs Headquarters, before the founding of the People's Republic of China. The building facade has a clear three-section structure, and all parts are in proper proportion, showing a typical Chinese and Western integrated feature. Its foundation steps are made of red sandstones, which are local specialties of western Sichuan. Walls and peripheral columns are made of black bricks. Front columns are original Greek columns, and rear ones are chamfered square columns, with excellent masonry technology. The building has a gable and hip roof, covered with Chinese-style tiles. On the left and right walls are porches. Thus, Western architectural style is integrated harmoniously with the local style in Chengdu. This building is a representative of well-conserved mansions in Chengdu in modern times. Currently it is used as the office of Sichuan Academy of Contemporary Oil Painting.

徐子昌旧居

FORMER RESIDENCE OF XU ZICHANG

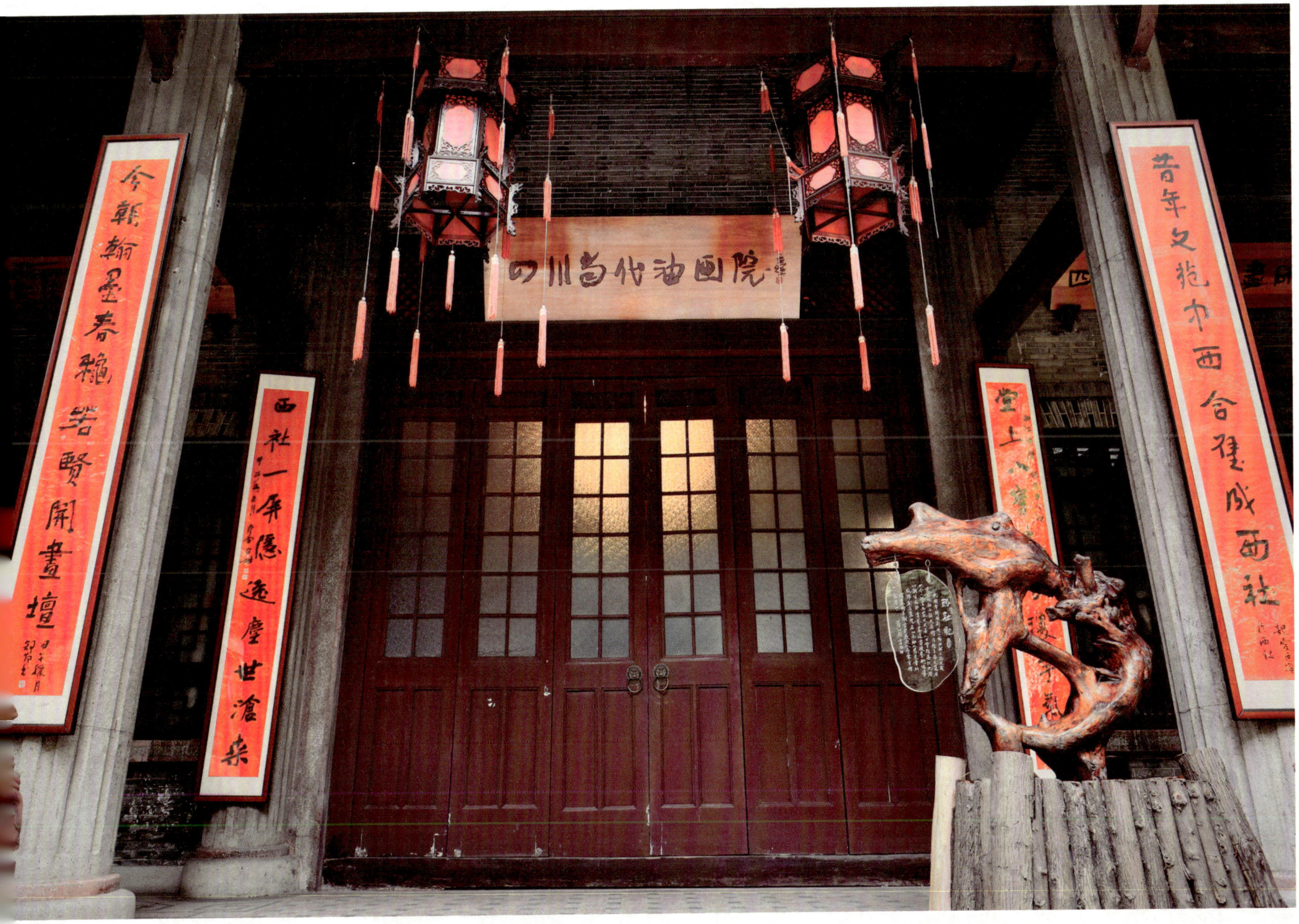

成都建筑·遗珠

CHENGDU ARCHITECTURE HERITAGE

CAMPUS

LIBRARIES AND

BUILDINGS

学苑馆室

自汉代文翁兴学

开创巴蜀崇文重教之先河

千百年来

成都人文蔚起

遍布蓉城大大小小的学苑馆堂

延续着巴蜀千载不绝的文脉

在古色古香、书声琅琅的院落里

夜色中走出的每一道身影

都气宇轩昂……

Wenweng established a school here in the Han Dynasty,
which started the respect for teaching and learning in Sichuan and Chongqing.
For about two thousand years,
the humanistic culture has been developing prosperously in Chengdu.
Schools in different sizes have spread all over the city,
extending the thousand-year-old vein of learning in Sichuan and Chongqing.
Each figure walking from the antique courtyards
with loud reading voices at nights
shows dignified bearing …

原四川大学女生院

民國

FORMER WOMEN'S COLLEGE OF SICHUAN UNIVERSITY

建筑名称：原四川大学女生院

建筑地址：四川大学望江校区内

建筑面积：1920 平方米

建筑年代：20 世纪 40 年代

Building Name: Former Women's College of Sichuan University

Location: InSichuan University Wangjiang Campus

Built-up Area: 1,920 square meters

Completion: In the 1940s

川西民居风格的三合院。1949 年后曾用作校长办公室和中共四川大学党委办公室，著名学者和教育家谢文炳、周太玄、彭迪先、温建平等均曾在此办公，也是"江姐"江竹筠在川大两年的生活地，具有浓厚的历史人文气息，是成都市内不可多得的建筑文化遗产。红门、青瓦、灰墙、精致的雕花，是川西近代校园建筑的重要历史遗存。原党办所在建筑现已被拆掉，校办建筑保留至今，现为四川大学中华文化研究院。

This building is a three-section compound of western Sichuan folk house style. It was once used as President's Office and the office of CPC Sichuan University Committee after the founding of the People's Republic of China (1949). Such famous scholars and educators as Xie Wenbing, Zhou Taixuan, Peng Dixian, and Wen Jianping once worked in this building. Jiang Zhujun, a famous Chinese revolutionary martyr, once lived here for two years. With a profound historical and cultural atmosphere, this building is a rarely-seen architectural cultural heritage in downtown Chengdu. With a red door, Chinese style tiles, grey walls, and delicate carved flowers, this building is an important heritage of campus building in western Sichuan in modern times. The building which was used as the office of CPC Sichuan University Committee before has been demolished. Only the building used as President Office before has remained and it is now used as Chinese Culture Research Institute of Sichuan University.

华西协合大学中国文化研究所旧址

民國

FORMER SITE OF CHINESE CULTURAL STUDIES RESEARCH INSTITUTE OF WEST CHINA UNION UNIVERSITY

建筑名称：华西协合大学中国文化研究所旧址

建筑地址：人民南路三段华西口腔医学院内

建筑面积：404 平方米

建筑年代：1940 年

Building Name: Former Site of Chinese Cultural Studies Research Institute of West China Union University

Location: In West China College of Stomatology, Sichuan University, Section 3, Renmin Road South

Built-up Area: 404 square meters

Completion: In 1940

该建筑曾是华西协合大学中国文化研究所的办公所在地，砖木结构，中西合璧风格，现属四川大学华西校区的公共建筑。在动荡的抗战时代，这里云集了闻宥、陈寅恪、吕叔湘、韩儒林、刘朝阳等海内外知名的顶尖学术大家，孕育出了《华西协合大学中国文化研究所论丛》《华西协合大学中国文化研究所集刊》等杰出学术刊物。它也曾作为华西协合大学宿舍楼使用，历史上先后有多位学术大家在此寓居，是 20 世纪 40 年代中国文化精英聚集的场所，被誉为“保存和延续中国高等教育和学术研究命脉的圣地之一”。修缮后的旧址将作为中国文化研究所旧址纪念馆向社会公众开放。

This building was once used as the office of Chinese Cultural Studies Research Institute of West China Union University, with a brick-timber structure of Chinese and western style. Now it is a public building at Sichuan University Huaxi Campus. During the War of Resistance Against Japanese Aggression, some well-known academic experts, including Wen You, Chen Yinke, Lyu Shuxiang, Han Rulin, and Liu Chaoyang, once worked here and some outstanding academic journals, such as the Essays of Chinese Cultural Studies Research Institute of West China Union University and the Collections of Chinese Cultural Studies Research Institute of West China Union University, were born here. This building was also used as a dorm building of West China Union University. Many academic experts once lived here one after another in history. Known as one of the holy places for conserving and continuing China's higher education and academic research lifeline, the building was a place where many Chinese cultural elites got together in the 1940s. After being renovated, this site opened to the public as a memorial hall for the Former Site of Chinese Cultural Studies Research Institute.

原华西协合大学校长楼

民國

PRESIDENT'S BUILDING OF FORMER WEST CHINA UNION UNIVERSITY

建筑名称：原华西协合大学校长楼

建筑地址：武侯区人民南路三段 17 号四川大学华西校区东区 8 号院

建筑面积：734.45 平方米

建筑年代：20 世纪 20 年代

Building Name: President's Building of Former West China Union University

Location: No. 8 Courtyard, East Area of Sichuan University Huaxi Campus, 17 Section 3, Renmin Road South, Wuhou District

Built-up Area: 734.45 square meters

Completion: In the 1920s

该建筑既有欧式建筑的青砖墙柱及拱形门洞、壁炉烟囱，又有川西建筑的小青瓦屋面、走马转角外廊，且两者结合自然巧妙，形成川西地区近现代住宅建筑的特有风格，是成都地区中西合璧建筑的经典之作，具有较高的建筑史学价值。华西协合大学校长毕启、张凌高曾在此居住，现属四川大学所有，为外宾楼。该建筑长期作为校长的住宅，是学校主要领导重要的活动场所，见证了华西协合大学和我国西部医学的发展历程。

This building has blue bricks and wall columns, arched door, fireplace, chimney of European-style buildings and also Chinese style tile roof and exterior corner corridor of Western Sichuan buildings, which are brought together subtly to form a particular style of modern residential buildings in western Sichuan. It is a masterpiece of Chinese and Western-style integrated building in Chengdu, with a high architectural historical value. Joseph Beech and Zhang Linggao, former presidents of West China Union University, once lived in this building, which is now owned by Sichuan University and used for foreign guests. This building used to be president's residence for a long period. As an important venue for activities for main leaders of the university, it witnessed the development of West China Union University and medical science in West China.

原华西协合大学
校长楼

PRESIDENT'S BUILDING OF FORMER
WEST CHINA UNION UNIVERSITY

八号院

四川大学 志德堂

ZHIDE HALL OF SICHUAN UNIVERSITY

建筑名称：四川大学志德堂

建筑地址：四川大学华西校区内

建筑面积：3430 平方米

建筑年代：20 世纪 20 年代

Building Name: Zhide Hall of Sichuan University

Location: In Sichuan University Huaxi Campus

Built-up Area: 3,430 square meters

Completion: In the 1920s

电信路
Dianxin Road
校西路
Xiaoxi Road
公行道
Gongxing Path

由英国著名建筑学家弗烈特·荣杜易（Fred Rowntree）设计。初为原华西协合大学加拿大学校（Canadian School），供在四川工作的外籍人士子女上学使用，后为华西公共卫生学院教学楼，俗称第七教学楼，“中国公共卫生之父”陈志潜曾在此办公。该建筑是四川大学华西校区中西合璧优秀建筑，是我国历史建筑瑰宝——原华西协合大学建筑群中的代表作，也是成都市最为重要的文化建筑、教育建筑遗存之一。

Zhide Hall of Sichuan University was designed by Fred Rowntree, a famous British architect. Initially, it was used as West China Union University's Canadian School, which was built for children of foreigners working in Sichuan. Later it was used as the teaching building of West China School of Public Health, known as No. 7 Teaching Building. Chen Zhiqian, the father of public health in China, once worked in this building. As an excellent building of Chinese and Western integrated style, this building is a representative of the former West China Union University building complex, which has been praised as a treasure of historical buildings in China. It is also one of the most important cultural buildings and education buildings existing in Chengdu.

四川大学
志德堂
民國

ZHIDE HALL OF
SICHUAN UNIVERSITY

四川大学
数 理 馆

MATHEMATICS AND SCIENCE BUILDING OF SICHUAN UNIVERSITY

建筑名称：四川大学数理馆

建筑地址：武侯区一环路南一段 24 号
四川大学望江校区内

建筑面积：3909.62 平方米

建筑年代：1941 年

Building Name: Mathematics and Science Building of Sichuan University

Location: In Sichuan University Wangjiang Campus, 24 Section 1, 1st Ring Road South, Wuhou District

Built-up Area: 3,909.62 square meters

Completion: In 1941

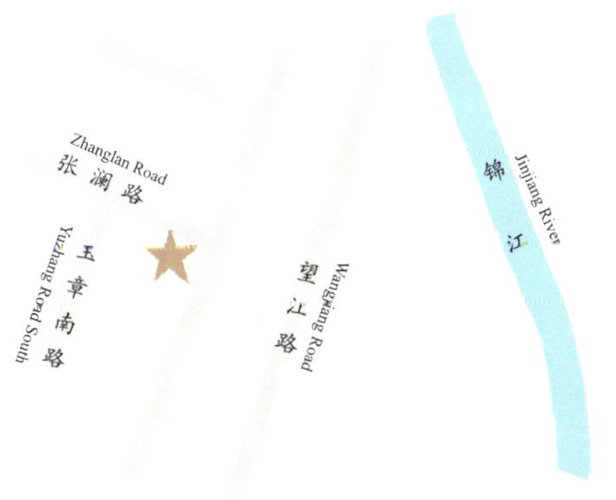

望江东区，听荷池畔，两幢砖木结构、形式相仿的现代中式建筑遥遥相望，它们由著名建筑大师杨廷宝设计，同属于当年国立四川大学最早修建的“三馆一舍”，其中一幢便是川大数理馆。三层高，坡屋顶，青筒瓦屋面，“T”字形布局，正入口居中，拥有美观气派的建筑体型与协调统一的比例尺度。1944 年川大定址望江新校区，数理馆交由川大数学、物理系学生使用，在历经院系调整与校院合并重组后，如今是川大物理科学与技术学院的办公及教学楼。

Two modern Chinese-style brick-timber buildings face each other from afar beside Tinghe Pool in the east area of Sichuan University Wangjiang Campus. Designed by Yang Tingbao, a famous master architect, these buildings belong to the earliest "three buildings and one dorm" built by National Sichuan University. One of them is Mathematics and Science Building of Sichuan University, which has three floors and a pitched roof covered with green pantiles. The building has a T-shaped layout, with entrance in the middle. It looks beautiful and splendid, with a harmonious ratio scale. When Sichuan University was sited at New Wangjiang Campus in 1944, the Mathematics and Science Building was used by the Department of Mathematics and the Department of Physics of Sichuan University for use. After department/college adjustment and restructuring, the building is now being used as the office and teaching building of the College of Physical Science and Technology of Sichuan University.

四川大学
化学馆

CHEMISTRY BUILDING OF
SICHUAN UNIVERSITY

滴海涵

建筑名称：四川大学化学馆

建筑地址：武侯区一环路南一段 24 号
四川大学望江校区内

建筑面积：4163.54 平方米

建筑年代：1941 年

Building Name: Chemistry Building of Sichuan University

Location: In Sichuan University Wangjiang Campus, 24 Section 1, 1st Ring Road South, Wuhou District

Built-up Area: 4,163.54 square meters

Completion: In 1941

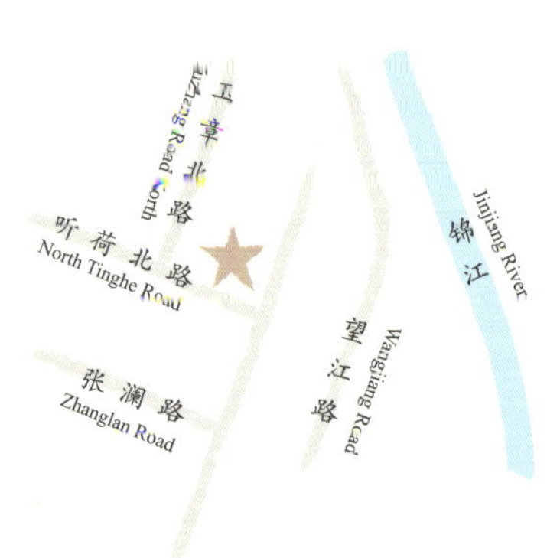

同样出自建筑大师杨廷宝之手的川大化学馆与数理馆相向而立。建筑整体呈现出中国近代教学楼建筑的特有风格，既有欧式建筑的墙柱、烟囱、老虎窗，又有川西建筑的青筒瓦屋面。每到秋季，红墙、青砖、灰瓦与楼前的银杏黄叶相映成趣，别具一番韵味。“寸草春晖，涓滴海涵”，春来秋去七十余年，化学馆未曾改变过其最初的主体结构、名称和用途。

The Chemistry Building of Sichuan University was also designed by Yang Tingbao, a famous master architect. It stands opposite to the Mathematics and Science Building of Sichuan University. As a whole, it shows a particular style of teaching buildings in China in modern times, with European-style wall columns, chimney, and dormant windows as well as western Sichuan-style green pantile roof. In each autumn, red walls, black bricks, Chinese style tiles, and yellow ginkgo leaves in front of the building form a delightful contrast, showing a special charm. “Parents’ and teachers’ love and care can hardly be reciprocated by their children and students”. Though 70 years have elapsed, the Chemistry Building’s original main structure, name and purpose have never changed.

该建筑具有欧式建筑雄伟庄重的特色，房屋造型独特、宏伟大气，极具美感，建筑比例适当，工艺精细，女儿墙栏杆装饰大气稳重，走廊及过厅内部空间舒适宜人，室内设计装饰精美。

This building has the majestic and unique characteristics of European architecture. The house is unique in shape and is magnificent. The building proportion is appropriate and the craftsmanship is fine. The parapet fences are magnificently decorated and dignified; the corridor and the interior space of the hall are comfortable and pleasant, and the interior is well designed and beautifully decorated.

电子科技大学沙河校区主楼

MAIN BUILDING AT UNIVERSITY OF ELECTRONIC SCIENCE AND TECHNOLOGY OF CHINA SHAHE CAMPUS

建筑名称：电子科技大学沙河校区主楼

建筑地址：成华区建设北路二段 4 号

建筑面积：26323 平方米

建筑年代：始建于 1956 年

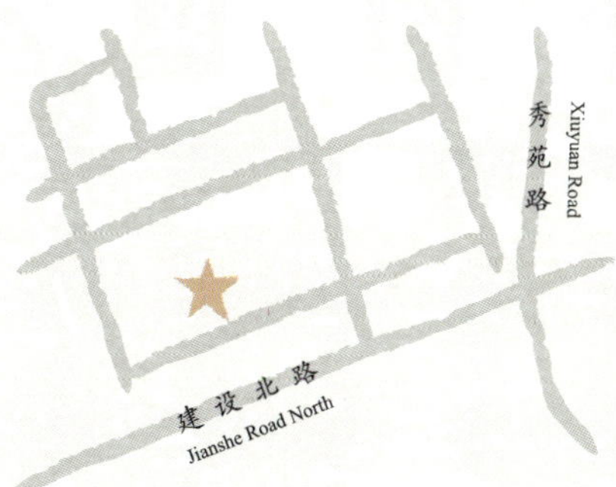

Building Name: Main Building at University of Electronic Science and Technology of China Shahe Campus

Location: 4 Section 2, Jianshe Road North, Chenghua District

Built-up Area: 26,323 square meters

Completion: Construction started in 1956

电子科技大学
沙河校区主楼

MAIN BUILDING AT UNIVERSITY OF
ELECTRONIC SCIENCE AND TECHNOLOGY
OF CHINA SHAHE CAMPUS

该建筑仿照苏联"莫洛托夫动力学院"教学主楼进行设计，占地面积7344平方米，坐西北朝东南，主楼楼体长223米，宽75米，总平面呈"凹"字形展开，正面主体建筑为5层苏式楼房，左右两侧各有连接纵向延伸的对称建筑。建筑为砖木结构，体量宏大、特色鲜明，是当时成都面积最大的单体建筑之一，承载着电子科技大学的办学历史和厚重的人文底蕴，也是电子科技大学发展历程和中苏友好关系的历史见证。目前主楼保存完好，仍作为沙河校区办公及教学大楼。

Modeled after the main building of the Molotov Power Academy of the former Soviet Union, this building covers an area of 7,344 square meters and its front faces the southeast. The main building body is 223 meters long and 75 meters wide. The general plan is in a "concave" shape. The front main building is a 5-storey Soviet-style building with symmetrical buildings extending longitudinally on the left and right sides. The building is in a brick-timber structure, with a large volume and distinctive features, as one of the largest single buildings in Chengdu at that time. It carries with it the teaching history and profound humanistic heritage of the University of Electronic Science and Technology of China, and the development history of the University of Electronic Science and Technology of China, and it is also a historical testimony of the Sino-Soviet friendship. This main building is now well preserved, still used as the office and teaching building at Shahe Campus.

通锦中学老宿舍楼

OLD DORMITORY BUILDING OF TONGJIN MIDDLE SCHOOL

建筑名称：通锦中学老宿舍楼

建筑地址：金牛区通锦路 15 号通锦中学校内

建筑面积：2790 平方米

建筑年代：1954 年

Building Name: Old Dormitory Building of Tongjin Middle School

Location: In Tongjin Middle School, 15 Tongjin Road, Jinniu District

Built-up Area: 2,790 square meters

Completion: In 1954

中国中铁二院

该建筑为苏式建筑风格，二楼一底砖木结构，是成都市内保存比较完整的20世纪50年代初期修建的校园建筑。学校原名"铁道部新建铁路工程总局成都职工子弟中学学校"，是成都地区创办最早的企业子弟中学，先后更名为"西南铁路局职工子弟中学校""铁道部第二铁路工程局成都第一子弟中学校"，2000年正式定名为"中铁二局一中"，2006年改名为"成都市通锦中学"。该建筑是成都新中国成立以来教育发展历史的见证。

This is a Soviet-style building of brick-timber structure, with one ground floor and two additional floors. Built in the early 1950s, it is a well-conserved campus building in Chengdu. Formerly, the school was named Middle School for Children of Chengdu Employees of New Railway Engineering Bureau under the Ministry of Railway, which was the earliest middle school that was built in Chengdu for children of enterprise employees. Later it was renamed Middle School for Children of Employees of Southwest China Railway Bureau, and then Chengdu No. 1 Middle School for Children of Employees of No. 2 Railway Engineering Bureau under the Ministry of Railways. In 2000, the school was named No. 1 Middle School of China Railway No. 2 Group. In 2006, it was renamed Chengdu Tongjin Middle School. This building witnessed the process of education development in Chengdu after the founding of the People's Republic of China.

成都中医药大学原行政办公楼

FORMER ADMINISTRATIVE BUILDING OF CHENGDU UNIVERSITY OF TCM

建筑名称：成都中医药大学原行政办公楼

建筑地址：金牛区十二桥街 37 号成都中医药大学内

建筑面积：5933.36 平方米

建筑年代：1954 年

Building Name: Former Administrative Building of Chengdu University of TCM

Location: In Chengdu University of TCM, 37 Shierqiao Street, Jinniu District

Built-up Area: 5,933.36 square meters

Completion: In 1954

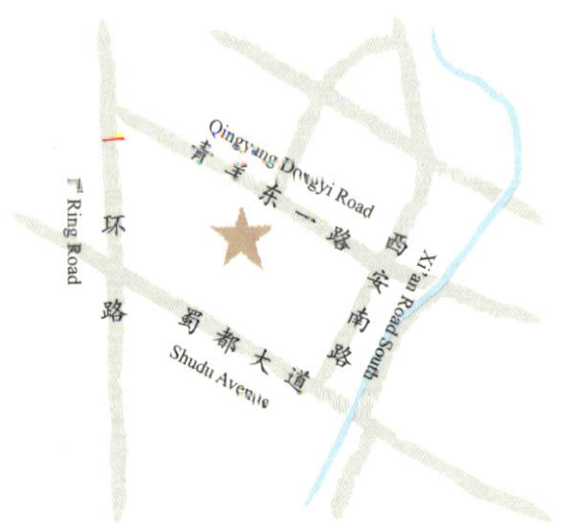

国医馆

成都中医药大学原行政办公楼

FORMER ADMINISTRATIVE BUILDING OF CHENGDU UNIVERSITY OF TCM

该建筑为三层砖木结构，平面规整，呈中轴左右对称布局，中间高两侧低，主楼高耸，回廊宽缓伸展，整体按檐部、墙身、勒脚呈三段式构图，比例美观大方，局部细节采用灰塑的山花及拱券门样式，保存较好，是建国初期成都校园建筑的代表之一。

This building is of a three-story brick-timber structure, with a regular plane and arranged symmetrically on the central axis. The middle part is high while both sides are low. The main building is towering, and the corridor extends widely and gently. The overall structure consists of three sections: entablature, wall and plinth, in a beautiful and graceful proportion layout. Lime-carving pediment and arches are displayed at some locations and are well preserved. It is one of the representatives of campus architecture in Chengdu built shortly after the founding of the People's Republic of China.

双流中学钟楼

BELL TOWER OF SHUANGLIU MIDDLE SCHOOL

建筑名称：双流中学钟楼

建筑地址：双流区广场路 39 号双流中学校园内

建筑面积：218.3 平方米

建筑年代：1949 年

Building Name: Bell Tower of Shuangliu Middle School

Location: In Shuangliu Middle School, 39 Guangchang Road, Shuangliu District

Built-up Area: 218.3 square meters

Completion: In 1949

双流中学创办于1940年，其内的钟楼是一座具有川西古典建筑风格的八角重檐楼宇，是该校仅存的标志性老建筑，为学校一景“钟楼流韵”。建筑占地面积180平方米，三层砖木结构，因最上层挂有一座大铁钟而得名，建筑主体保存完整，造型古朴典雅，工艺考究，对研究近代楼阁建筑具有一定价值。曾作为校长办公室、校务会议室、教室、实验室、师生寝室等，1996年3月修缮后用作校史陈列室，并沿用至今，对研究双流中学校史及双流教育历史具有重要意义。

Shuangliu Middle School was established in 1940. The bell tower in the school is an octagonal double-eave building with a classical western Sichuan architectural style. As the only survival of landmark old buildings in the school, the tower has become a landscape in the campus. Covering a land area of 180 square meters, the tower has a three-storey brick-timber structure. It was named so because there is a big iron bell at the top of the tower. The principal part of the tower is well conserved. Its shape is simple, unsophisticated, and elegant, and its craftsmanship is excellent. This tower has a certain value for the study of storied buildings in modern times. It was once used as Headmaster's Office, meeting room, classroom, lab, and dorm for teachers and students. Since it was repaired in March 1996, it has been used as the school's showroom. It is of great significance to the research of Shuangliu Middle School's history and Shuangliu's education history.

双流中学钟楼

BELL TOWER OF SHUANGLIU MIDDLE SCHOOL

成都建筑·遗珠

CHENGDU ARCHITECTURE HERITAGE

FACTORIES, MILLS AND TEAHOUSES

厂坊茶市

"蓉城茗楼如春笋，清风飘来茉莉香"
这是巴蜀人民的草根活法
守一杯淡茶浓茶
便知回归与传承构筑的乡土情缘
亲情友情人情世故的底线
滚烫的茶水冲泡
生活的烟火升起
盆地对每个人来说都是家园……

"Teahouses in Chengdu are like bamboo shoots in springs; fragrance of jasmine tea floats with refreshing breeze".
It is a lifestyle of common people in Sichuan and Chongqing:
with a cup of strong or light tea,
one may experience the homelike feelings of return and inheritance
and know the bottom line of family love, friendship and worldly wisdom.
Making tea in boiling hot water,
smoke rising from kitchen chimneys,
Sichuan Basin is the home of all people here …

广东会馆

GUANGDONG GUILD HALL

建筑名称：广东会馆

建筑地址：锦江区大慈寺街区

建筑面积：1300 平方米

建筑年代：民国初年

Building Name: Guangdong Guild Hall

Location: In the Dacisi Block, Jinjiang District

Built-up Area: 1,300 square meters

Completion: In the early Republic of China

广东会馆
GUANGDONG GUILD HALL

该会馆由清代移民四川的广东籍人士集资兴建，曾是成都地区广东籍同乡的聚会场所。现建筑为民国初年修建，会馆呈四合院布局，木抬梁和穿逗结构，硬山屋面，建筑造型别致，漆饰恢宏，陶雕、木雕、石雕工艺精湛，具有岭南建筑风格，承载着“湖广填四川”这一重要历史事件的宝贵记忆，也是研究广东籍商人社会生活的样本。现为太古里街区内商业展览、文化交流场所。

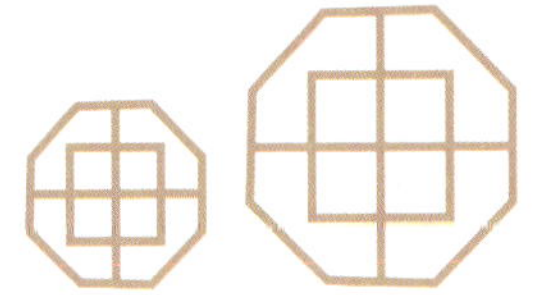

This guild hall was built by Guangdong emigrants in Sichuan in the Qing Dynasty, and used to be a meeting place for Guangdong emigrants in Chengdu. The existing building was built in the early years of the Republic of China. It is a quadrangle courtyard layout, with wooden post and lintel, and column and tie construction, and Chinese gabled roofs. The architectural style is unique; the lacquer decoration is magnificent; the craftsmanship of pottery, wood and stone carving is exquisite. It is with the architectural style of Guangxi and Guangdong and carries forward the precious memory of the important historic event of "Huguang people filling Sichuan". It is also a sample to study the social life of Guangdong businessmen, and is now used as a site for business exhibition and cultural exchange in Taikoo Li Block.

广东会馆

GUANGDONG GUILD HALL

白药厂旧址

FORMER SITE OF GUNPOWDER FACTORY

建筑名称：白药厂旧址

建筑地址：武侯区高攀路 26 号

建筑面积：1846.93 平方米

建筑年代：1906 年

Building Name: Former Site of Gunpowder Factory

Location: 26 Gaopan Road, Wuhou District

Built-up Area: 1,846.93 square meters

Completion: In 1906

白药厂旧址

FORMER SITE OF GUNPOWDER FACTORY

白药厂是清政府在四川最早设立的军工厂，在当时专为四川机器局提供火药而建，是洋务运动时期典型的工业建筑，也是成都地区仅存的清末工业建筑群。建厂初期有建筑数十幢，现存行政楼、装具车间、钳工车间等十余栋建筑，其中四栋为清末建筑，其余皆为 20 世纪 80 年代后陆续修建。整个建筑群多为砖木混合结构，木屋架坡屋顶，融合了中西方建筑特色。这些镌刻着工业文明发展进程的老工业遗迹，记载了成都城市发展的历史，也折射出中国近代军事工业发展的轨迹。

The gunpowder factory was the earliest ordnance factory established by the Qing government in Sichuan Province, dedicated to providing gunpowder to Sichuan Machinery Bureau at that time. It is a typical industrial building during the Westernization Movement and the only remaining industrial cluster from the Qing Dynasty in Chengdu. Upon its launch, there were dozens of buildings, a dozen or so of which still exist now, including the administrative building, the equipment workshop, and the bench worker workshop. Four of them are buildings constructed in the late Qing Dynasty, and the rest of them were built during and after the 1980s. The entire building complex is mostly of brick-timber mixed structures, with wooden roof truss and pitched roofs, integrating the characteristics of Chinese and Western architectures. These old industrial relics engraved with footprints of industrial civilization have recorded history of Chengdu's urban development and also reflected the development track of China's modern military industry.

BY 1906
YOUNG 创意工厂
成都
武侯区
高攀路26号
爱国
赤诚
献
1876
源起

FORMER SITE OF
GUNPOWDER FACTORY

观音阁老茶馆

OLD TEAHOUSE IN GUANYIN PAVILION

建筑名称：观音阁老茶馆

建筑地址：双流县彭镇马市坝街 64 号

建筑面积：220 平方米

建筑年代：清代

Building Name: Old Teahouse in Guanyin Pavilion

Location: 64 Mashiba Street, Pengzhen Town, Shuangliu County

Built-up Area: 220 square meters

Completion: In the Qing Dynasty

茶馆为木梁青瓦老平房，墙壁上斑驳的毛主席头像和标语口号残存着『文革』时期的记忆。

This teahouse is an old single-story house with wooden beams and Chiese style tiles. The mottled portrait of Chairman Mao and slogans on the wall display residual memories of the Cultural Revolution.

始建于明中后期，初为观音庙，民国初期改为茶馆，故名“观音阁老茶馆”。“文革”时期作为会场，至今保留该时期风貌，存有诸多“文革”宣传画、标语等。建筑为全木架构，分为两部分，前半部分茶馆主体采用川西民居传统穿逗结构，后半部分为20世纪70年代搭建。整体保存较好，是研究四川民俗文化的实证，也是老成都茶文化的重要载体。同时，该建筑保留的“文革”记忆，是特殊历史时期的缩影，也是珍贵的历史文化遗产。现仍作为茶馆经营，传承老成都独有的茶馆文化。

Originally built in the middle and late Ming Dynasty, this building used to be a Guanyin Temple. It was changed into a teahouse in the early Republic of China, hence the name “Old Teahouse in Guanyin Pavilion”. During the Cultural Revolution, this building was used as a venue, and it now still retains the style of that period, with many Cultural Revolution posters and slogans. This building is of a fully-wooden structure, divided into two parts. The main part of the teahouse in the first half is in the traditional column and tie construction of West Sichuan folk houses, and the second half was built in the 1970s. It is well preserved as a whole, and is an empirical example for studying Sichuan folk culture and an important carrier of the old Chengdu tea culture. Besides, the memory of the Cultural Revolution preserved by this building is a microcosm of a special historical period and a precious historical and cultural heritage. It is still operating as a teahouse and carries forward the unique teahouse culture of old Chengdu.

老茶馆至今仍维持着几十年前简单朴素的生活气息，仿若时光在此停滞，茶杯中沉淀着历史。

An easy and simple lifestyle decades ago still remains in the old teahouse, as if the time is stagnant here and the history settles down in the teacup.

观音阁老茶馆

OLD TEAHOUSE IN GUANYIN PAVILION

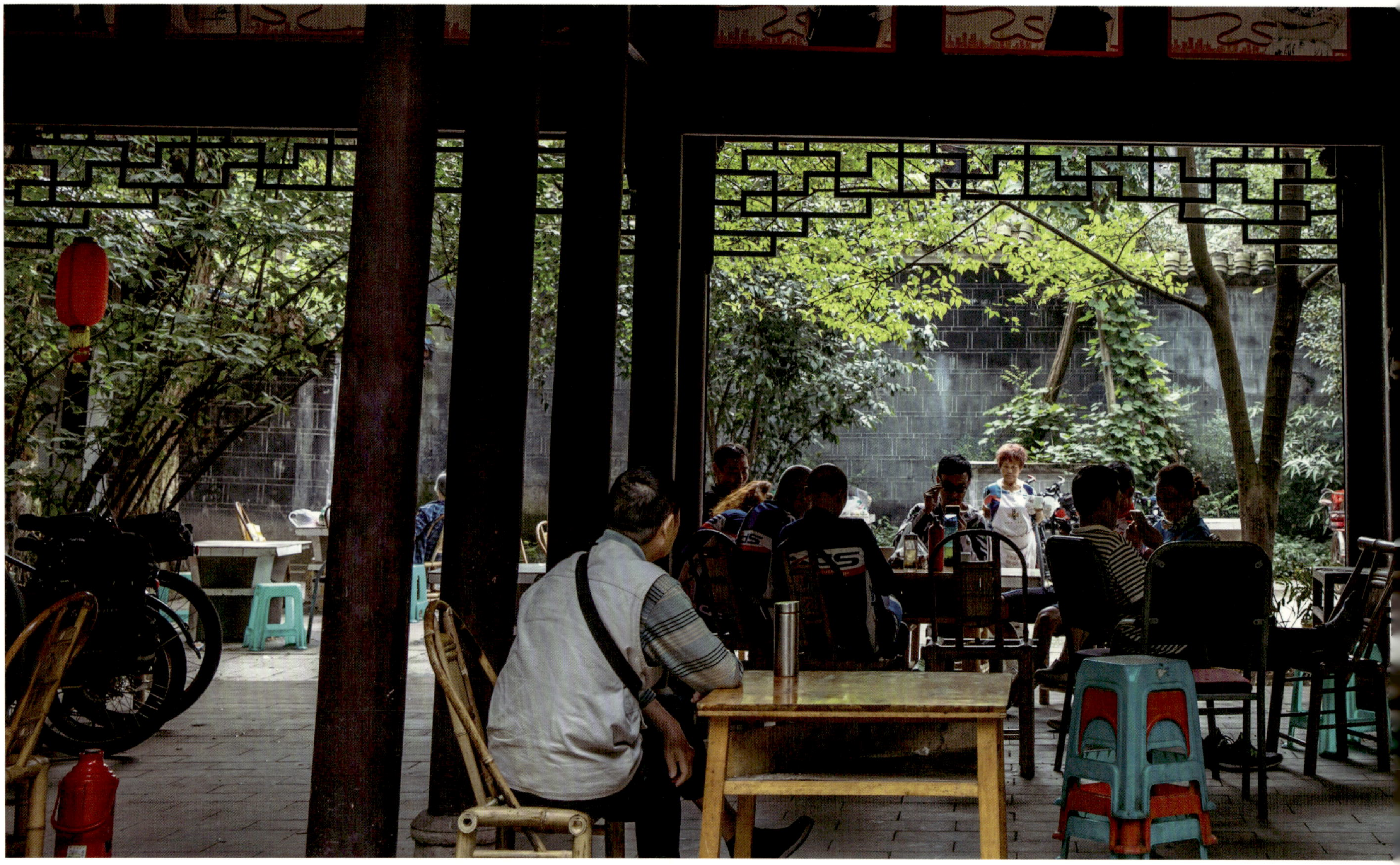

民國

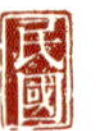

崇宁公园茶楼

TEAHOUSE IN
CHONGNING PARK

茶楼掩映在碧绿的树木中，满池青翠的浮萍与之相映，构建出别样幽静安宁的氛围。

The teahouse sits amid green trees, against the tender duckweeds packed in the pond, creating a unique tranquil and peaceful atmosphere.

建筑名称：崇宁公园茶楼

建筑地址：郫县唐昌镇公园路 27 号崇宁公园内

建筑面积：500 平方米

建筑年代：1927 年

Building Name: Teahouse in Chongning Park

Location: In Chongning Park, 27 Gongyuan Road, Tangchang Town, Pixian County

Built-up Area: 500 square meters

Completion: In 1927

崇宁公园茶楼

TEAHOUSE IN CHONGNING PARK

崇宁公园相传为明代崇宁王府后花园，现建筑是民国时期所建，为两层木质小楼，建筑形式独特、结构精巧、造型优美，兼具实用性与艺术性，具有民国时期川西园林建筑特点，是崇宁公园内仅存的民国时期木结构建筑，是唐昌镇保留完整、富有特色的传统建筑之一。建筑整体形制保存较好，现作为茶楼使用，环境清幽、景色宜人。

Chongning Park was said to be the back garden of Prince Chongning Mansion in the Ming Dynasty. The existing building was built during the Republic of China and is a two-story wooden building. The architectural form is unique, with an exquisite structure and beautiful shapes, both practical and artistic. It is with the characteristics of West Sichuan garden architecture during the Republic of China, and is the only wooden structure that has survived from the Republic of China in the Chongning Park and one of the completely preserved and most traditional buildings in Tangchang Town. The overall shape of the building is well preserved, and it is now used as a teahouse, characterized by a quiet environment and its charming scenery.

崇宁公园茶楼

TEAHOUSE IN
CHONGNING PARK

鹤鸣茶社

HEMING TEAHOUSE

建筑名称：鹤鸣茶社

建筑地址：人民公园内

建筑面积：/

建筑年代：1908 年

Building Name: Heming Teahouse

Location: In People's Park

Built-up Area: /

Completion: In 1908

鹤鸣茶社
HEMING TEAHOUSE

该建筑位于成都老城区近代最早的公园——“少城公园”内，因茶社的开创者为龚姓大邑商人，故名“鹤鸣茶社”。为局部两层楼榭亭廊，布局自由的川西传统园林建筑，民国时期少城公园内六大茶馆之首，历来为文化名人雅集之所。1949年前，鹤鸣茶社的主要茶客为教师与公职人员，是信息汇集、人才招聘集中之所，是“六腊战争”主战场，也是目前成都主城区所有茶馆中历史最久、影响最大的茶馆，亦是中国茶文化中的地标性文化场所之一。现在的鹤鸣茶社由沿湖长廊、院坝和主楼三部分组成，长廊和主楼经多次修缮，保留完好。茶社内的雕塑墙、老虎灶、茶叶店、叶圣陶诗碑等，均展现着原汁原味的老成都茶文化风貌。

The building is located in Shaocheng Park, the earliest park in the old urban area of Chengdu in modern times. Since the founder of the building is a businessman from Dayi, whose surname is Gong, the building was named Heming Teahouse. As a western Sichuan traditional garden building with two floors, it ranked first among top six teahouses in Shaocheng Park during the period of the Republic of China. Cultural celebrities frequently meet at this teahouse. Before 1949, customers of Heming Teahouse were mainly teachers and civil servants. As a result, the teahouse became a source of information and a personnel recruitment place. It was also a main battlefield of the “June and December War”. Now it is the oldest and most influential teahouse in downtown Chengdu and one of the landmarks of Chinese tea culture. Today’s Heming Teahouse is made up of three parts, i.e. riverside corridor, courtyard, and main building. Undergoing repeated repairs, the corridor and main building are reserved well. The sculpture wall, dormant kitchen range, tea shop, and Ye Shengtao poem tablet in the teahouse reflect the original flavor of old Chengdu tea culture.

锦江宾馆

JINJIANG HOTEL

建筑名称：锦江宾馆

建筑地址：锦江区人民南路二段 80 号

建筑面积：40613.66 平方米

建筑年代：建于 1958 年，1960 年完工

Building Name: Jinjiang Hotel

Location: 80 Section 2, Renmin Road South, Jinjiang District

Built-up Area: 40,613.66 square meters

Completion: In 1960 (construction started in 1958)

锦江宾馆
JINJIANG HOTEL

锦江宾馆坐落于成都市主干道人民南路，毗邻府南河，环境条件优越，是西南地区首家五星级酒店，由成都籍中国建筑大师徐尚志设计，朱德和陈毅两位川籍老帅亲自选定“锦江”一词定名，是成都市 20 世纪中期地标建筑代表。建筑为现代建筑风格，造型气派大方，体量组合稳重均衡，立面处理简洁明快，色彩运用协调自然。2016 年 9 月 29 日，锦江宾馆被中国文物学会、中国建筑学会公布为“首批中国 20 世纪建筑遗产”。

Located beside Renmin Road South, a trunk road in Chengdu, Jinjiang Hotel neighbors the Funan River, enjoying excellent environmental conditions. As the first five-star hotel in southwest China, Jinjiang Hotel was designed by Xu Shangzhi, a Chinese master architect who was born in Chengdu, and named by Zhu De and Chen Yi (two noted Sichuan-born marshals). It was a representative landmark building in Chengdu in the mid-20th century. With a modern architectural style, Jinjiang Hotel looks splendid, generous, steady and balanced. Its façade is concise and lively, with harmonious and natural colors. On September 29, 2016, Jinjiang Hotel was put on the list of the "First Batch of Architectural Heritages in China in the 20th Century" by China Cultural Relics Academy and the Architectural Society of China.

JINJIANG
HOTEL

原成都机车车辆厂灯光球场

FORMER FLOODLIT COURT OF CHENGDU ROLLING STOCK PLANT

建筑名称：原成都机车车辆厂灯光球场

建筑地址：成华区二仙桥街道市民活动中心内

建筑面积：1436.31 平方米

建筑年代：1979 年

Building Name: Former Floodlit Court of Chengdu Rolling Stock Plant

Location: In the Citizen Activity Center, Erxianqiao Sub-district, Chenghua District

Built-up Area: 1,436.31square meters

Completion: In 1979

价值观 培育向上向善向美的社区精神
大力弘扬中华优秀传统文化 塑造二仙辖区特色文化品牌

灯光球场是成都机车车辆厂基于人防和职工娱乐两个需求，耗时3年，动员全厂上下数千职工修建而成，为环形、钢筋混凝土结构综合性建筑，包括球场、地下活动室及人防工程，球场呈圆形，直径约40米，1987年之前为地下游乐场地，后废弃，现由二仙桥街道市民活动中心使用。作为成都市工业遗产，它反映了特定历史时期产业工人的生产生活方式，见证了成都工业发展的进程，是工业文明的重要遗存。

In order to meet the two demands, i.e. civil air defense and staff entertainment, the court was built by thousands of employees of Chengdu Rolling Stock Plant through three years' efforts. As a circular integrated building with a reinforced concrete structure, it is made up of court, underground activity room, and civil air defense works. With a round shape, the court is about 40m in diameter. Before 1987, there was an underground pleasure ground, which was abandoned later. Now the court is used as the Citizen Activity Center of Erxianqiao Sub-district. As Chengdu's industrial heritage, it has reflected industrial workers' mode of production and lifestyle in a specific historical period and witnessed the process of industrial development in Chengdu. It is important remains of industrial civilization.

原成都机车车辆厂灯光球场

FORMER FLOODLIT COURT OF CHENGDU ROLLING STOCK PLANT

原四川省青城造纸厂厂房

FACTORY BUILDING OF FORMER SICHUAN QINGCHENG PAPER MILL

建筑名称：原四川省青城造纸厂厂房

建筑地址：都江堰市壹街区玉垒路 51 号

建筑面积：5928.6 平方米

建筑年代：20 世纪 80 年代

Building Name: Factory Building of Former Sichuan Qingcheng Paper Mill

Location: 51 Yulei Road, Yijiequ Block, Dujiangyan City

Built-up Area: 5,928.6 square meters

Completion: In the 1980s

上善西路
Shangshan Road West
玉垒路
Yulei Road

原四川省青城造纸厂厂房

FACTORY BUILDING OF FORMER SICHUAN QINGCHENG PAPER MILL

原为青城造纸厂厂房，“5·12”特大地震后由上海对口援建，同济大学建筑设计院采用“建筑再生”设计理念，在青城造纸厂原厂房基础上，重新设计建设而成，尽可能保留原有厂房的一些构件和设施，包括牛腿、吊车梁、部分机械设备等。现为国家一级图书馆，分为两个区，以保留的厂房为主体，在原厂房空间利用轻钢结构加建两层楼面，作为借书、阅览场所；与厂房主楼转折相接的是新建的报告厅副楼，两个区形成一长一短、一新一旧的“Y”字形布局。该建筑使图书馆既留下了工业文明的城市记忆，又注入了精神文化重建的新内涵，是上海人民和都江堰人民历史、情感、文化的见证和延续。

The factory building of former Qingcheng Paper Mill was rebuilt on the original foundation with the help of Shanghai after the May 12th great earthquake. It was designed by the Architectural Design and Research Institute of Tongji University according to the concept of “architectural regeneration”. Structures and facilities of original factory building, including bracket, crane beam, machine and equipment, were maximally retained. Now the building is used as a national level-1 library, including two areas. Based on the retained factory building, a two-storey steel-structure building was built additionally in the original space of factory buildings. It is used as a place for book borrowing and reading. A newly-built annex building of Lecture Hall connects the main building of factory buildings at the turning point. Two areas form a Y-shaped layout, with one being long and new while the other one being short and old. The library contains not only urban memory of industrial civilization but also new connotations of spiritual culture reconstruction. It witnessed and continues the history, emotion, and culture of Shanghai people and Dujiangyan people.

依托明月窑成立的明月国际陶艺村，现为以陶艺为主的手工创意聚集区，已打造成陶瓷文化旅游地。

Mingyue International Ceramics Village was established by relying on Mingyue Kiln. Now it is a handcraft creativity concentration zone focusing on ceramic arts, and has been built into a ceramic culture tourist attraction.

明月窑

MINGYUE KILN

建筑名称：明月窑

建筑地址：蒲江县甘溪镇明月村12组

建筑面积：100平方米

建筑年代：清代

Building Name: Mingyue Kiln

Location: Group 12, Mingyue Village, Ganxi Town, Pujiang County

Built-up Area: 100 square meters

Completion: In the Qing Dynasty

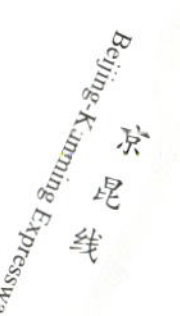

明月窑

MINGYUE KILN

该窑为原上张碗厂窑址，始建于清康熙年间，属阶梯形龙窑，占地面积400平方米，砖砌体结构，总长19.5米，宽5.5米，以土砖、泥土等材料依一定的坡度倾斜砌筑，由窑门、火膛、七个单独窑仓和烟囱组成。各室相连而独立，从下至上一仓高于一仓，形成层层阶梯，形制浑朴，万状有致。明月窑在“5·12”特大地震前300余年从未断烧，是还在进行生产的“活着的古窑”。地震受损停产后，于2014年初夏，重新开窑，这座百年老窑再次焕发新春，现属明月村12组集体所有，作为邛窑遗址参观。

Built duringthe reign of Emperor Kangxi in the Qing Dynasty, Mingyue Kiln used to be a kiln of former Shangzhang Bowl Factory. As a stepped dragon kiln, it covers a land area of 400 square meters. Built with bricks and soils, it is 19.5m in length and 5.5m in width, with a certain gradient. It is comprised of a door, a hearth, seven separate kiln bins, and a chimney. Each bin is independent and also joins each other. All spaces line up orderly from bottom to top, with steps on each layer. During the 300 years before the May 12th earthquake, the operation of Mingyue Kiln was never discontinued. It is a "living ancient kiln" in use today. Due to the May 12th earthquake, production of Mingyue Kiln paused. In early summer of 2014, the 100-year-old kiln was opened again. Now the kiln is owned collectively by villagers of Group 12, Mingyue Village, and, as a site of Qionglai kiln, opened to visitors.

成都建筑·遗珠

CHENGDU ARCHITECTURE HERITAGE

大厦楼堂

BUILDINGS AND MANSIONS

沿旧楼房寻昔日荣光

谋划长远铸今朝辉煌

每一块砖都饱含废寝忘食呕心沥血

多少白天夜晚殚精竭虑为苍生计

才换来蜀道之难天堑变通途

才换来古城新都人才荟萃百川归海

才换来蓉城“来了就不想走”的美名流传……

Walking along the old buildings to explore their past glory,

forefathers' long-term plans create today's brilliance.

The glory of every brick derives from forefathers' painstaking efforts.

How many days and nights were exhausted for the sake of the common people,

so that the tough Sichuan roads have become a thoroughfare,

so that this ancient city has gathered talents from across the world

so that Chengdu has gained the reputation of "a place that you don't want to leave once you come" …

原中共成都市委办公楼群（5、6、8号楼）

FORMER OFFICE BUILDING COMPLEX OF CPC CHENGDU MUNICIPAL COMMITTEE (BUILDINGS NO. 5, NO. 6, AND NO. 8)

建筑名称：原中共成都市委办公楼群（5、6、8号楼）

建筑地址：青羊区羊市街19号

建筑面积：5205.17平方米

建筑年代：20世纪30年代

Building Name: Former Office Building Complex of CPC Chengdu Municipal Committee (Buildings No. 5, No. 6, and No. 8)

Location: 19 Yangshi Street, Qingyang District

Built-up Area: 5,205.17 square meters

Completion: In the 1930s

20 世纪三四十年代，该建筑群是天主教会本笃会和赎世主会主要活动地之一，50 年代初期作为成都市委主要领导和机关办公区使用，直至 2011 年。现是成都市第三人民医院南扩建筑群中的一部分，5、6 号楼为门诊部，8 号楼为成都市第一家医药博物馆。建筑是中西合璧式的风格，对东西方宗教文化交流和成都的建设发展产生过重要影响。

In the 1930s and 1940s, this building complex was one of the main venues of St Benedict's Catholics and the Holy Redeemer Church. In the early 1950s, it was used as the office by main leaders and departments of CPC Chengdu Municipal Committee, until 2011. Now it is a part of southwards-expanded buildings of Chengdu No. 3 People's Hospital. No. 5 and 6 Buildings are used for Outpatient Department while No. 8 Building used as a Pharmacy Museum. With a Chinese and Western integrated style, this building complex has had an important effect on the exchange of Eastern and Western religious culture as well as the development of Chengdu.

原中共成都市委办公楼群
（5、6、8 号楼）

FORMER OFFICE BUILDING COMPLEX OF CPC CHENGDU MUNICIPAL COMMITTEE (BUILDINGS NO. 5, NO. 6, AND NO. 8)

原中共成都市委办公楼群（5、6、8号楼）
Former Office Building Complex of CPC Chengdu Municipal Committee (Buildings No. 5, No. 6, and No. 8)

SERVICE CENTER

原成都市政府办公楼

FORMER OFFICE BUILDING OF CHENGDU MUNICIPAL GOVERNMENT

建筑名称：原成都市政府办公楼

建筑地址：青羊区人民西路 2 号

建筑面积：9638 平方米

建筑年代：1956 年

Building Name: Former Office Building of Chengdu Municipal Government

Location: 2 Renmin Road West, Qingyang District

Built-up Area: 9,638 square meters

Completion: In 1956

原成都市政府办公楼

FORMER OFFICE BUILDING OF CHENGDU MUNICIPAL GOVERNMENT

原成都市政府办公楼

FORMER OFFICE BUILDING OF CHENGDU MUNICIPAL GOVERNMENT

该建筑由四川省建筑设计院设计，砖木结构，屋顶为平坡结合，坡屋顶为木屋架、小青瓦屋面，有办公用房及会议室191间。该楼建成至2010年，一直作为市政府办公楼使用，现由市公安局出入境管理局和市人民政府外事办使用，分别有市公安局出入境管理局、市出入境接待中心、市人民政府外事服务中心、友好城市展厅、出国管理处等单位在此办公。该建筑见证了新中国成立以来成都的城市建设发展历程，是天府广场标志性建筑物之一。

With a brick-timber structure, this building was designed by Sichuan Provincial Architectural Design and Research Institute. It has both flat and pitched roofs. Pitched roofs are made of timber and covered with Chinese-style tiles. There are 191 office rooms and meeting rooms. The building was used as the office building of Chengdu Municipal Government until 2010. Now it is used as the offices for the Exit and Entry Administration Division of Chengdu Municipal Public Security Bureau and the Foreign Affairs Office of Chengdu Municipal Government. Many departments, including the Exit and Entry Administration Division of Chengdu Municipal Public Security Bureau, the Reception Center of the Exit and Entry Administration Division, the Foreign Affairs Service Center of Chengdu Municipal Government, the Exhibition Hall of Sister Cities, and the Overseas Visits Administration, perform official business in this building. As one of landmark buildings in Tianfu Square, this building has witnessed the process of urban development in Chengdu since the founding of the People's Republic of China.

省经信委办公楼

OFFICE BUILDING OF SICHUAN PROVINCIAL ECONOMIC AND INFORMATION COMMISSION

建筑名称：省经信委办公楼

建筑地址：青羊区人民东路 66 号

建筑面积：6991.19 平方米

建筑年代：1956 年

Building Name: Office Building of Sichuan Provincial Economic and Information Commission

Location: 66 Renmin Road East, Qingyang District

Built-up Area: 6,991.19 square meters

Completion: In 1956

学党章党规 学系列讲话

四川省煤炭工业管理办公室
四川煤矿安全监察局
四川省安全生产监督管理局
四川省人民政府安全生产委员会办公室
四川省经济和信息化委员会
四川省中小企业局
四川省信息化工作办公室

省经信委办公楼

OFFICE BUILDING OF SICHUAN PROVINCIAL ECONOMIC AND INFORMATION COMMISSION

该建筑原址为明代城墙所在地，建筑为多层砖木混合建筑，平面规整，呈中轴左右对称布局，整体按檐部、墙身、勒脚呈三段式构图，比例美观大方，属于带苏式建筑风格的现代建筑。现用于省经济和信息委员会办公，属省机关事务管理局所有。该建筑是天府广场标志性建筑物之一，是中华人民共和国成立后一段特殊历史时期的重要建筑遗存，见证了中华人民共和国成立以来成都城市建设发展历程。

This building was built at the location of city walls built in the Ming Dynasty. Most houses are multi-storey brick-timber mixed houses and laid out symmetrically in the right and left of the axis. As a whole, the building has three parts, i.e. entablature, wall body, and plinth, which are in a perfect proportion. It belongs to a modern building of Soviet architectural style. Now it is used as the offices of Sichuan Provincial Economic and Information Commission and owned by Sichuan Provincial Government Offices Administration. As a landmark building in Tianfu Square, this building is important building remains that were built in a special historical period after the founding of the People's Republic of China. It witnessed the process of urban development in Chengdu after the founding of the People's Republic of China.

原金堂县县政府大门

ENTRANCE OF FORMER JINTANG COUNTY GOVERNMENT

建筑名称：原金堂县县政府大门

建筑地址：青白江区城厢镇槐树街社区西街 10 号

建筑面积：/

建筑年代：民国时期

Building Name: Entrance of Former Jintang County Government

Location: 10 West Street, Huaishujie Community, Chengxiang Town, Qingbaijiang District

Built-up Area: /

Completion: During the Republic of China

堂縣縣政

ENTRANCE OF FORMER JINTANG
COUNTY GOVERNMENT

原金堂县县政府大门

ENTRANCE OF FORMER JINTANG COUNTY GOVERNMENT

原为清代金堂县衙大门所在，1930年（民国十九年），县衙改为金堂县政府，大门亦重新修建，政府各职能办事机构均设置于内。中华人民共和国成立初始，因机构调整，县政府迁走，改建为城厢幼儿园。现仅存大门保存较好，属国有。该构筑物见证了城厢镇作为民国时期金堂县县政府驻地的历史，为研究地方历史提供了实物资料，并且融合了中西建筑特色，是研究古代衙署向近代政府类建筑转变的实物例证。

Formerly, it was the entrance of Jintang County Government in the Qing Dynasty. In 1930 (the 19th year during the Republic of China), it was rebuilt and all government offices were set inside. Soon after the founding of the People's Republic of China, it was rebuilt into Chengxiang Kindergarten due to adjustment of government offices and relocation of the County Government. Now only the entrance remains and it is a state-owned property. It witnessed the history of Chengxiang Town serving as the county seat of Jintang County during the period of the Republic of China. It provides physical materials to the study of local history and shows both Chinese and Western architectural features. It is a physical example for studying the transformation of ancient government offices into modern government buildings.

中国建筑西南设计研究院有限公司旧办公楼

OLD OFFICE BUILDING OF CHINA SOUTHWEST ARCHITECTURAL DESIGN AND RESEARCH INSTITUTE CORP., LTD.

建筑名称：中国建筑西南设计研究院有限公司旧办公楼

建筑地址：金牛区星辉西路 8 号院内

建筑面积：7091 平方米（不含地下室）

建筑年代：1957 年

Building Name: Old Office Building of China Southwest Architectural Design and Research Institute Corp., Ltd.

Location: In No. 8 Courtyard, Xinghui Road West, Jinniu District

Built-up Area: 7,091 square meters (excluding basement)

Completion: In 1957

成都中医大银海眼科医院

中国建筑西南设计研究院有限公司旧办公楼

OLD OFFICE BUILDING OF CHINA SOUTHWEST ARCHITECTURAL DESIGN AND RESEARCH INSTITUTE CORP., LTD.

该建筑是我国中西部最大的建筑设计院——中国建筑西南设计研究院50多年的办公场所，是20世纪50年代成都办公建筑中较为成功的实例，由成都籍著名建筑大师徐尚志设计，是成都市第一座新型的办公楼，见证了中西部地区乃至全中国城市建设的发展历史。建筑特色鲜明，建筑风格既非当时流行的仿苏式风格，也非传统建筑风格，而是在体现新时代建筑理念的基础上，融入了传统建筑的符号和元素，在新中国建筑史上占据了一席之地。

This building has been used as the office by China Southwest Architectural Design and Research Institute, the largest architectural design and research institute in Midwest China, for more than 50 years. As an example of successful office building in Chengdu in the 1950s, it was designed by Xu Shangzhi, a famous architect born in Chengdu. As Chengdu's first new-type office building, it witnessed the development of urban buildings in Midwest China or even throughout the country. This building has a distinguishing architectural feature. Its architectural style is neither then-popular Soviet style nor traditional architectural style. Based on reflecting new-era building concepts, this building contains signs and elements of traditional buildings. It has played an important role in the architectural history of new China.

原西南铁路工程局通信楼

COMMUNICATION BUILDING OF FORMER SOUTHWEST RAILWAY ENGINEERING BUREAU

建筑名称：原西南铁路工程局通信楼

建筑地址：金牛区通锦路 13 号

建筑面积：680.95 平方米

建筑年代：1955 年

Building Name: Communication Building of Former Southwest Railway Engineering Bureau

Location: 13 Tongjin Road, Jinniu District

Built-up Area: 680.95 square meters

Completion: In 1955

原西南铁路工程局通信楼

COMMUNICATION BUILDING OF FORMER SOUTHWEST RAILWAY ENGINEERING BUREAU

该建筑为两层砖木结构，平面规整，呈中轴左右对称布局，中间高两侧低，主楼高耸，回廊宽缓伸展，整体按檐部、墙身、勒脚呈三段式构图，比例美观大方，属于带苏式建筑风格的现代建筑，保存较好，体现出该历史时期建造技术水平。作为原西南铁路工程局的生产调度通信指挥中枢，参与了对成昆铁路、湘黔铁路、成渝铁路、宝成铁路等重要国家战略项目的调度指挥，见证了我国西南铁路事业的发展历程。现属中铁二局集团股份有限公司（原铁道部第二铁路工程局）所有，中铁二局集团电务股份有限公司用于办公。

With a two-storey brick-timber structure, this building is in good order in terms of plane layout. Its left part and right part are symmetrical along the axis. The middle part is higher than both sides. The main building stands tall and erect while the corridor stretches up gradually. Generally it is comprised of three sections, i.e. entablature, wall body, and plinth, which are in a perfect proportion. It belongs to a modern building of Soviet architectural style. Currently it is conserved well, showing the level of construction technology in that period. The building was once used as a production dispatching and commanding hub of former Southwest Railway Engineering Bureau to serve such national strategic projects as Chengdu-Kunming Railway, Hunan-Guizhou Railway, Chengdu-Chongqing Railway, and Baoji-Chengdu Railway. It witnessed the development of railway industry in southwest China. Now the building is owned by China Railway No. 2 Group Co., Ltd. (formerly No. 2 Railway Engineering Bureau of the Ministry of Railways) and used as the office by the Electrical Engineering Co., Ltd. of China Railway No. 2 Group.

成都建筑·遗珠

CHENGDU ARCHITECTURE

HERITAGE

桥梁津渡

BRIDGES AND AQUEDUCTS

江水润泽天府
河桥密布巴蜀
一座座桥梁犹如历史坐标
见证成都与水千丝万缕的关系
谱一曲水旱从人
谱一曲花重锦城
谱一曲茶马古道汉藏情谊深
桥承载着千载传唱的蜀水文化
“门泊东吴万里船”的仓廪底气
守望着悠悠蜀江波影……

River water moistens the Land of Abundance,
and bridges are scattered over bridges in Sichuan and Chongqing.
Bridges are like historical coordinates,
witnessing the countless ties between Chengdu and water.
Here, floods and droughts are under the easy control of the humans;
here, flowers hang heavy in the Embroidered Official City;
here, the ancient Tea-Horse Road demonstrates the profound friendship between Han people and Tibetans.
Bridges carry with them the thousand-year-extolled Shu water culture,
and the material foundation of "by the door moor ships from Eastern Wu ten thousand miles away",
and guard the leisurely waves of rivers in Sichuan ...

南桥

SOUTH BRIDGE

建筑名称：南桥

建筑地址：都江堰市灌口街道办离堆公园大门北侧

建筑面积：1080 平方米

建筑年代：始建于清代

Building Name: South Bridge

Location: North of the entrance of Lidui Park, Guankou Sub-district Office, Dujiangyan City

Built-up Area: 1,080 square meters

Completion: Construction started in the Qing Dynasty

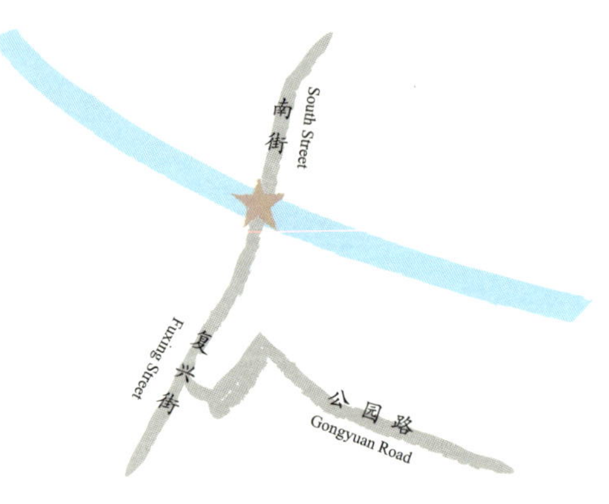

南桥属廊式古桥，四墩五孔，长 65.8 米，宽 12.8 米，南北朝向，整体由桥墩、桥梁、桥面以及桥上廊房构成。两侧桥头为三重歇山屋顶，桥头楼阁飞檐凌空，重檐彩绘鲜艳夺目，屋顶的民间传说与人物彩塑，情态各具，栩栩如生。桥面铺板，两旁设栏，形成长廊式走道，主走廊内壁上精工绘制二十幅山水风景和神话传说壁画与十八幅书法作品相间排列。南桥系历史名桥，经过一百多年的维护和修缮，被誉为"天府第一桥"、"水上画楼"、"雄踞江源第一桥"等，位于世界遗产都江堰核心景区，反映了李冰治水的人文精神内核。

As an ancient covered bridge, South Bridge has four piers and five openings. It is 65.8m in length and 12.8m in width, running from north to south. The bridge is comprised of piers, beams, bridge floor, and corridor room on the bridge. There is a gable and hip roof at both sides of the bridge, with pavilions and overhanging eaves. Double eaves are painted with an eye-catching color. On the roof are vivid figures in folklore, showing different expressions. Boards are paved on the bridge floor and guardrails are set at both sides to form a corridor-like walkway. On the internal wall of main corridor, there are 20 beautiful landscape pictures and portraitures of figures from myths and legends as well as 18 pieces of calligraphy works. South Bridge has a history of more than 100 years. It has been maintained and repaired many times. Located in the core area of Dujiangyan Scenic Spot, a world heritage site, South Bridge has been praised as the Best Bridge in Sichuan, the Overwater Painting Building, the First Bridge at the River Source etc. It reflects the essence of the humanistic spirit of Li Bing's efforts to control rivers and watercourses.

夹关镇解放渡槽

LIBERATION AQUEDUCT IN JIAGUAN TOWN

建筑名称：夹关镇解放渡槽

建筑地址：邛崃市夹关镇拴马村 8、9 组

建筑面积：1000 平方米

建筑年代：20 世纪 70 年代

Building Name: Liberation Aqueduct in Jiaguan Town

Location: Groups 8 and 9, Shuanma Village, Jiaguan Town, Qionglai City

Built-up Area: 1,000 square meters

Completion: In the 1970s

该渡槽是邛崃五绵山支渠上段跨夹关河（南河支流）的一座水利工程，外观高大雄伟，具有水利灌溉的重要功能。西北—东南走向，总长 320 米，为 8 跨钢筋混凝土拱形结构，每跨 35 米；槽身为矩形，槽底净宽 2.4 米，墙高 2.3 米，槽身顶部左侧内悬人行桥，寿高公路从渡槽下穿过，渡槽内水源是从青衣江支流玉溪河上筑坝引水而来，可灌溉芦山、邛崃、名山、蒲江四县（市）境内 58 万亩土地和供部分支渠周边人口饮用。渡槽修建牢固，历经近半个世纪依旧完好稳定，沿用至今。

This aqueduct is a water conservancy project crossing the Jiaguan River (a tributary of the Nanhe River) in the upper section of Wumianshan Branch Canal in Qionglai. It looks majestic, with important irrigation functions. Running from the northwest to the southeast, the aqueduct is 320m in length, with eight reinforced concrete arches. Each arch has a span of 35m. The aqueduct takes on a rectangular look. The bottom of the aqueduct is 2.4m in net width. The wall is 2.3m in height. A pedestrian bridge is suspended in the left side at the top of the aqueduct. Shougao Highway crosses below the aqueduct. Water in the aqueduct comes from a dam on the Yuxi River, a tributary of the Qingyi River. It is used to irrigate 580,000mu (some 386,860,000 square meters) land in four counties, i.e. Lushan, Qionglai, Mingshan and Pujiang Counties, and as drinking water for residents living near some tributaries. Since the aqueduct was firmly built, it is still in good condition and in use today, half a century after its completion.

大同乡 景沟廊桥  JINGGOU COVERED BRIDGE IN DATONG TOWNSHIP

建筑名称：大同乡景沟廊桥

建筑地址：邛崃市大同乡景沟村1组

建筑面积：30平方米

建筑年代：民国二十八年（1939年）

Building Name: Jinggou Covered Bridge in Datong Township

Location: Group 1, Jinggou Village, Datong Township, Qionglai City

Built-up Area: 30 square meters

Completion: In the 28th year during the Republic of China (1939)

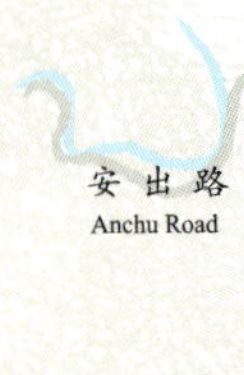

大同乡 景沟廊桥

民国

JINGGOU COVERED BRIDGE IN DATONG TOWNSHIP

原名为“金风桥”，为周姓乡绅修建，经时代变迁更名为“景沟廊桥”，是当时茶马古道上的一处重要通道，为来往商旅提供了交通便利。该建筑为石木质结构，横卧河面，桥面为红砂石板，桥下两个石拱相连，桥长11.6米、宽3.4米，桥廊为木穿逗结构，两侧各砌10根沙木立柱，重檐歇山屋顶，屋顶为青瓦铺盖，两端飞檐翘角，装饰朴素大方得体，桥头立一观音碑。该建筑对于研究当地交通发展历史和茶马古道文化具有重要意义。

Formerly known as the “Jinfeng Bridge”, this bridge was built by a country gentleman surnamed Zhou, and its name has eventually evolved into the “Jinggou Covered Bridge”. It used to be an important passage on the ancient Tea-Horse Road, providing convenient transportation for businessmen and travelers. This building is of a stone and wood structure, lying horizontally above the river. Its surface consists of red sandstone slates, and two stone arches are connected at its bottom. With a length of 11.6m and a width of 3.4m, the bridge has a corridor of timber column and tie construction, and 10 fir columns each stand on both sides. The double-eaved, gable and hip roof is covered with Chinese style tiles, with cornices on both ends. The decoration is plain and graceful, with a Mercy Buddha stele at the end of bridge. The building is of great significance for studying the history of local transportation development and the culture of the ancient Tea-Horse Road.

后记

EPILOGUE

《诗经·国风·卫风》："如切如磋，如琢如磨。"回顾《成都建筑·遗珠Ⅰ》一书的创作过程，从构思框架、议定提纲、罗列文献资料、筛选材料、反复斟酌修订，到点位踩点、拍摄，再到编辑出版，离不开各位参编人员长期繁琐而艰辛的工作，更离不开各位领导、专家学者高度重视、关注和鼎力支持。同时，对给予本项工作大力支持的成都市房管局谨致以由衷的感谢。

《成都建筑·遗珠Ⅰ》中建筑均来自成都市人民政府公布的《成都市历史建筑保护名录》（第一批—第十一批），本书共收录50处建筑，排名不分先后。另外，成都市一些为人熟知的著名历史建筑不在该名录之中，这部分建筑已被纳入国家级、省级重点保护建筑名单予以保护，而公布的《成都市历史建筑保护名录》中的建筑多是处于边缘地带、甚至濒危的建筑物。希望通过本书的出版，将成都市这些鲜为人知的建筑遗存珍宝亮相于众。

习近平主席曾指出，"历史文化是城市的灵魂，要像爱惜自己的生命一样保护好城市历史文化遗产。"走在开放前沿，冲刺世界城市，生机勃勃的新成都更需要城市历史文化的衬托。将成都历史建筑的前世今生带到读者眼前，展现出成都建筑深厚的历史背景和背后所蕴含的价值，让成都城市改造发展的历程能在此得窥一隅，实属编者的荣幸。同时也希望借此契机，助力成都建设世界文化名城并探索具有人文价值的城市可持续发展研究的新路径。

因客观条件及编者水平所限，本书若有遗漏或不当之处，恳请批评指正。

编 者

2018年11月18日

The *Book of Songs* suggests that people should help each other to make improvement. In the process of publishing this book – *Chengdu Architecture • Heritage I*, from conception, determination of outlines, listing and screening of related documents, revision, on-the-spot investigation, photography, to editing and publishing, all participants have made unremitting efforts in the past several months. Many leaders, experts and scholars have also attached great importance and greatly supported the publishing of this book. Sincere thanks also go to Chengdu Municipal House Property Administration for its great support.

The buildings introduced in *Chengdu Architecture • Heritage I* all come from the *List of Protected Historic Buildings in Chengdu* (Batches 1-11) published by Chengdu Municipal People's Government. This book introduces 50 buildings, which are listed in no particular order. In addition, some well-known historical buildings in Chengdu are not covered in this list because they have been included in the list of national and provincial-level protected buildings for the purpose of protection. Most buildings introduced in the *List of Protected Historic Buildings in Chengdu* are buildings that are in the edge zone or even in imminent danger. It is hoped that the publishing of this book may help more people learn about these little-known architectural treasures in Chengdu.

As pointed out by President Xi Jinping, "history and culture are the soul of a city. We must properly protect the historical and cultural heritage of the city just as we cherish our own lives." Walking in the forefront of opening-up and striving to be an international city, the new and vibrant Chengdu needs more its history and culture as its foundation. It is a great honor for the author to bring the past and present of Chengdu's historical buildings to in front of the readers' eyes, show the profound historical background of Chengdu's architecture and the value behind it, so that readers may briefly learn about the process of Chengdu's urban transformation and development. Also with this opportunity, some contributions may be made to help Chengdu build a world cultural city and explore a new research path for urban sustainable development with humanistic values.

Due to objective conditions and limited knowledge, if there is any omission or improper information in this book, please point it out. Thank you!

Author

November 18, 2018

成都市历史建筑保护名录（第一批—第十一批）

LIST OF PROTECTED HISTORIC BUILDINGS IN CHENGDU (BATCHES 1-11)

序号 Serial No.	名称 Name	位置 Location
1	邱家祠堂 Qiu's Ancestral Shrine	锦江区龙王庙正街 41 号 41 Longwangmiao Central Street, Jinjiang District
2	康季鸿公馆 Kang Jihong's Mansion	锦江区通盈街 699 号 699 Tongying Street, Jinjiang District
3	冯家大院 Feng's Grand Courtyard	青羊区九思巷 3 号 3 Jiusi Alley, Qingyang District
4	鹤鸣茶社 Heming Teahouse	青羊区少城路 12 号人民公园内 In People's Park, 12 Shaocheng Road, Qingyang District
5	原中共成都市委办公楼群（5、6、8 号楼） Former Office Building Complex of CPC Chengdu Municipal Committee (Buildings No. 5, No. 6, and No. 8)	青羊区羊市街 19 号大院内 In No. 19 Courtyard, Yangshi Street, Qingyang District
6	原成都市政府办公楼 Former Office Building of Chengdu Municipal Government	青羊区人民西路 2 号 2 Renmin Road West, Qingyang District
7	薛公馆 Xue's Mansion	金牛区解放路北一段 15 号 15 North Section 1, Jiefang Road, Jinniu District
8	张大千故居 Former Residence of Zhang Daqian	金牛区金泉路 2 号金牛宾馆内 In Jinniu Hotel, 2 Jinquan Road, Jinniu District
9	原成都电子机械高等专科学校办公楼 Office Building of Former Chengdu Electromechanical College	金牛区花牌坊街 2 号 2 Huapaifang Street, Jinniu District
10	欣庐 Xinlu Building	大慈寺街区内 In the Dacisi Block
11	笔帖式街老宅院 Old Courtyard House on Bitieshi Street	大慈寺片区内笔帖式街 Bitieshi Street in the Dacisi Block
12	崇德里民居 Chongdeli Folk House	红石柱横街 Hongshizhu Cross Street
13	原四川大学女生院 Former Women's College of Sichuan University	望江路 29 号川大望江校区内 In Sichuan University Wangjiang Campus, 29 Wangjiang Road
14	四川大学志德堂 Zhide Hall of Sichuan University	武侯区人民南路三段 17 号四川大学华西校区内 In Sichuan University Huaxi Campus, 17 Section 3, Renmin Road South, Wuhou District
15	华西协合大学中国文化研究所旧址 Former Site of Chinese Cultural Studies Research Institute of West China Union University	武侯区人民南路三段 14 号华西口腔医学院内 In West China College of Stomatology, Sichuan University, 14 Section 3, Renmin Road South, Wuhou District
16	谢无量旧居 Former Residence of Xie Wuliang	锦江区四圣祠西街 44 号 44 Sishengci Street West, Jinjiang District
17	总府路 81 号民居 Folk House at 81 Zongfu Road	锦江区总府路 81 号 81 Zongfu Road, Jinjiang District
18	龙王庙正街 70 号民居 Folk House at 70 Longwangmiao Central Street	锦江区龙王庙正街 70 号 70 Longwangmiao Central Street, Jinjiang District

序号 Serial No.	名称 Name	位置 Location
19	守经街6号民居 Folk House at 6 Shoujing Street	青羊区守经街6号 6 Shoujing Street, Qingyang District
20	中国建筑西南设计研究院有限公司旧办公楼 Old Office Building of China Southwest Architectural Design and Research Institute Corp., Ltd.	金牛区星辉西路8号院内 In No. 8 Courtyard, Xinghui Road West, Jinniu District
21	通锦中学老宿舍楼 Old Dormitory Building of Tongjin Middle School	金牛区通锦路15号通锦中学校内 In Tongjin Middle School, 15 Tongjin Road, Jinniu District
22	隆兴街42号民居 Folk House at 42 Longxing Street	锦江区隆兴街42号 42 Longxing Street, Jinjiang District
23	红石柱横街10号四合院 Quadrangle Courtyard at 10 Hongshizhu Cross Street	锦江区红石柱横街10号 10 Hongshizhu Cross Street, Jinjiang District
24	广东会馆 Guangdong Guild Hall	锦江区大慈寺街区 Dacisi Block, Jinjiang District
25	章华里老宅院 Zhanghuali Old Courtyard House	锦江区大慈寺街区 Dacisi Block, Jinjiang District
26	马家巷老宅院 Old Courtyard House on Majia Alley	锦江区大慈寺街区 Dacisi Block, Jinjiang District
27	谢家大院 Xie's Grand Courtyard	龙泉驿区茶店镇胜利村10组 Group 10, Shengli Village, Chadian Town, Longquanyi District
28	邓公楼 Deng's Mansion	青白江区城厢镇朝阳路社区公园路34号 34 Gongyuan Road, Chaoyang Road Community, Chengxiang Town, Qingbaijiang District
29	杨氏宗祠 Yang's Ancestral Shrine	新都区马家镇杨家村 Yangjia Village, Majia Town, Xindu District
30	王光祈旧居 Former Residence of Wang Guangqi	温江区柳城街道东街社区社学巷6号 6 Shexue Alley, East Street Community, Liucheng Sub-district, Wenjiang District
31	董寿平旧居 Former Residence of Dong Shouping	都江堰市西街122、124号 122 and 124 West Street, Dujiangyan City
32	赵连武宅 Zhao Lianwu's Mansion	彭州市新兴镇海窝子社区瞿上街 Qushang Street, Haiwozi Community, Xinxing Town, Pengzhou City
33	元通镇双凤街 Shuangfeng Street in Yuantong Town	崇州市元通镇双凤街2、4号民居 No. 2 and No. 4 Folk Houses, Shuangfeng Street, Yuantong Town, Chongzhou City
34	陈家大院 Chen's Grand Courtyard	邛崃市高何镇高兴村5组 Group 5, Gaoxing Village, Gaohe Town, Qionglai City
35	贺家大院 He's Grand Courtyard	金堂县五凤镇金箱村 Jinxiang Village, Wufeng Town, Jintang County
36	观音阁老茶馆 Old Teahouse in Guanyin Pavilion	双流区彭镇马市坝街64号 64 Mashiba Street, Pengzhen Town, Shuangliu County

序号 Serial No.	名称 Name	位置 Location
37	崇宁公园茶楼 Teahouse in Chongning Park	郫县唐昌镇公园路27号崇宁公园内 In Chongning Park, 27 Gongyuan Road, Tangchang Town, Pixian County
38	伍培英公馆 Wu Peiying's Mansion	大邑县邮江镇新街32号 32 New Street, Chujiang Town, Dayi County
39	余家编老宅院 Old Courtyard House at Yujiapian	蒲江县光明乡金花村余家编 Yujiapian, Jinhua Village, Guangming Township, Pujiang County
40	邓氏祖宅 Deng's Ancestral House	新津县邓双镇六水门街221号 221 Liushuimen Street, Dengshuang Town, Xinjin County
41	润居 Runju House	锦江区耿家巷37号 37 Gengjia Alley, Jinjiang District
42	双槐树街21号民居 Folk House at 21 Shuanghuaishu Street	锦江区双槐树街21号 21 Shuanghuaishu Street, Jinjiang District
43	四川省立第一甲种工业学校旧址 Former Site of Sichuan Provincial 1st Type A Technical School	青羊区包家巷82号 82 Baojia Alley, Qingyang District
44	谢无圻公馆 Xie Wuqi's Mansion	青羊区包家巷99号 99 Baojia Alley, Qingyang District
45	德盛路7号民居 Folk House at 7 Desheng Road	青羊区德盛路7号 7 Desheng Road, Qiangyang District
46	巫氏大夫第 Wu's Official Mansion	龙泉驿区洛带镇下街105号 105 Xiajie Street, Luodai Town, Longquanyi District
47	刘氏宗祠 Liu's Ancestral Shrine	新都区斑竹园镇三河村5组 Group 5, Sanhe Village, Banzhuyuan Town, Xindu District
48	双流中学钟楼 Bell Tower of Shuangliu Middle School	双流区广场路39号双流中学校园内 In Shuangliu Middle School, 39 Guangchang Road, Shuangliu District
49	都江堰西街104号附10号民居 Folk House at 104-10 West Street, Dujiangyan	都江堰市西街104号附10号 104-10 West Street, Dujiangyan City
50	裕盛长 Yushengchang Building	彭州市新兴镇梯云街67号 67 Tiyun Street, Xinxing Town, Pengzhou City
51	赵家祠堂 Zhao's Ancestral Shrine	邛崃市南宝山镇新桥村6组 Group 6, Xinqiao Village, Nanbaoshan Town, Qionglai City
52	元通镇半边街90号民居 Folk House at 90 Banbian Street, Yuantong Town	崇州市元通镇半边街90号 90 Banbian Street, Yuantong Town, Chongzhou City
53	省经信委办公楼 Office Building of Sichuan Provincial Economic and Information Commission	青羊区人民东路66号 66 Renmin Road East, Qingyang District
54	原西南铁路工程局通信楼 Communication Building of Former Southwest Railway Engineering Bureau	金牛区通锦路13号 13 Tongjin Road, Jinniu District
55	成都中医药大学原行政办公楼 Former Administrative Building of Chengdu University of TCM	金牛区十二桥街37号成都中医药大学内 In Chengdu University of TCM, 37 Shierqiao Street, Jinniu District
56	苏继贤旧居 Former Residence of Walter Small	武侯区人民南路17号四川大学华西校区内 In Sichuan University Huaxi Campus, 17 Renmin Road South, Wuhou District

序号 Serial No.	名称 Name	位置 Location
57	下河边街22、24号民居 Folk House at 22 and 24 Xiahebian Street	天府新区正兴镇苏码头社区下河边街22、24号 22 and 24 Xiahebian Street, Sumatou Community, Zhengxing Town, Tianfu New Area
58	水浸坝曾家寨子 Zeng's Stockaded Village at Shuijinba	青白江区城厢镇前锋村13组 Group 13, Qianfeng Village, Chengxiang Town, Qingbaijiang District
59	严家院子黄氏民居 Huang's Folk House at Yan's Courtyard	温江区寿安镇长青村15组 Group 15, Changqing Village, Shou'an Town, Wenjiang District
60	卜家院 Shijia Courtyard	崇州市怀远镇下新街63—73号 63-73 Xiaxin Street, Huaiyuan Town, Chongzhou City
61	宋家木楼 Song's Wooden Building	崇州市怀远镇上西街31号 31 Shangxi Street, Huaiyuan Town, Chongzhou City
62	林家大院 Lin's Grand Courtyard	崇州市怀远镇西江门街6号 6 Jiangmen Street West, Huaiyuan Town, Chongzhou City
63	杨公馆 Yang's Mansion	郫县唐昌镇文山路93号唐昌幼儿园内 In Tangchang Kingdergarten, 93 Wenshan Road, Tangchang Town, Pixian County
64	贺麟故居 Former Residence of He Lin	金堂县五凤镇金箱村2组 Group 2, Jinxiang Village, Wufeng Town, Jintang County
65	侯宝斋故居 Former Residence of Hou Baozhai	新津县花源镇洪川村12组 Group 12, Hongchuan Village, Huayuan Town, Xinjin County
66	李育滋公馆 Li Yuzi's Mansion	大邑县安仁镇新团村2组 Group 2, Xintuan Village, Anren Town, Dayi County
67	西来镇文风街111号民居 Folk House at 111 Wenfeng Street, Xilai Town	蒲江县西来镇文风街111号 111 Wenfeng Street, Xilai Town, Pujiang County
68	锦江宾馆 Jinjiang Hotel	锦江区人民南路二段80号 80 Section 2, Renmin Road South, Jinjiang District
69	谢无量旧居 Former Residence of Xie Wuliang	锦江区四圣祠西街36号附3号 36-3 Sishengci Street West, Jinjiang District
70	原华西协合大学校长楼 President's Building of Former West China Union University	武侯区人民南路三段17号四川大学华西校区东区8号院 No. 8 Courtyard, East Area of Sichuan University Huaxi Campus, 17 Section 3, Renmin Road South, Wuhou District
71	十二中街4号民居 Folk House at 4 Shier Zhongjie Street	武侯区十二中街4号 4 Shier Zhongjie Street, Wuhou District
72	徐子昌旧居 Former Residence of Xu Zichang	金牛区花牌坊街2号成都工业学院内 In Chengdu Technological University, 2 Huapaifang Street, Jinniu District
73	江源巷2号民居 Folk House at 2 Jiangyuan Alley	金牛区江源巷2号 2 Jiangyuan Alley, Jinniu District
74	龙王镇刘氏祠堂 Liu's Ancestral Shrine in Longwang Town	青白江区龙王镇梁湾村7组、12组 Groups 7 and 12, Liangwan Village, Longwang Town, Qingbaijiang District
75	石板滩镇文昌宫 Wenchang Palace in Shibantan Town	新都区石板滩镇正兴街126号 126 Zhengxing Street, Shibantan Town, Xindu District
76	石桥镇张家祠堂 Zhang's Ancestral Shrine in Shiqiao Town	简阳市石桥镇和平街55号 55 Heping Street, Shiqiao Town, Jianyang City
77	怀远镇小北街18号民居 Folk House at 18 Xiaobeijie Street, Huaiyuan Town	崇州市怀远镇小北街18号 18 Xiaobeijie Street, Huaiyuan Town, Chongzhou City

序号 Serial No.	名称 Name	位置 Location
78	平桥粮仓 Pingqiao Granary	金堂县平桥乡兴平街 1 号 1 Xingping Street, Pingqiao Township, Jintang County
79	四川机器局碉楼 Watchtower of Sichuan Machinery Bureau	锦江区三官堂街 31 号附 1 号 31-1 Sanguantang Street, Jinjiang District
80	"五·七"干校旧址 Former Site of May Seventh Cadres School	金牛区蓉都大道 1120 号 1120 Rongdu Avenue, Jinniu District
81	白药厂旧址 Former Site of Gunpowder Factory	武侯区高攀路 26 号 26 Gaopan Road, Wuhou District
82	空军制氧厂旧址 Former Site of Air Force Oxygen Plant	武侯区成双大道北段 509 号 509 North Section, Chengshuang Avenue, Wuhou District
83	原成都机车车辆厂灯光球场 Former Floodlit Court of Chengdu Rolling Stock Plant	成华区二仙桥街道市民活动中心内 In the Citizen Activity Center, Erxianqiao Sub-district, Chenghua District
84	柏合镇钟家大瓦房 Zhong's Tile-roofed House in Baihe Town	龙泉驿区柏合镇二河村 3 组 Group 3, Erhe Village, Baihe Town, Longquanyi District
85	和盛镇陈公馆 Chen's Mansion in Hesheng Town	温江区和盛镇舒家渡社区大桐街 Datong Street, Shujiadu Community, Hesheng Town, Wenjiang District
86	永安镇付家祠堂 Fu's Ancestral Shrine in Yongan Town	双流区永安镇付家坝社区 2 组 Group 2, Fujiaba Community, Yong'an Town, Shuangliu District
87	古井院 Ancient Well Courtyard	郫都区古城镇蜀汉中街 36 号 36 Middle Shuhan Street, Gucheng Town, Pidu District
88	南桥 South Bridge	都江堰市灌口街道办离堆公园大门北侧 North of the Entrance of Lidui Park, Guankou Sub-district Office, Dujiangyan City
89	弓明成宅 Gong Mingcheng's Mansion	彭州市天彭镇小南街 17 号 17 Xiaonan Street, Tianpeng Town, Pengzhou City
90	水口镇叶氏宗祠 Ye's Ancestral Shrine in Shuikou Town	邛崃市水口镇钟山社区 13 组 Group 13, Zhongshan Community, Shuikou Town, Qionglai City
91	廖维公馆 Liao Wei's Mansion	大邑县安仁镇金井村 5 社 Group 5, Jinjing Village, Anren Town, Dayi County
92	李家钰故居 Former Residence of Li Jiayu	蒲江县大兴镇炉坪村 3 组 Group 3, Luping Village, Daxing Town, Pujiang County
93	高升客栈 Gaosheng Inn	新津县花桥镇解放街 144 号 144 Jiefang Street, Huaqiao Town, Xinjin County
94	启庐 Qi Lu Building	锦江区新开街 84 号 84 Xinkai Street, Jinjiang District
95	电子科技大学沙河校区主楼 Main Building at University of Electronic Science and Technology of China Shahe Campus	成华区建设北路二段 4 号 4 Section 2, Jianshe Road North, Chenghua District
96	四川大学数理馆 Mathematics and Science Building of Sichuan University	武侯区一环路南一段 24 号四川大学望江校区内 In Sichuan University Wangjiang Campus, 24 Section 1, 1st Ring Road South, Wuhou District
97	四川大学化学馆 Chemistry Building of Sichuan University	武侯区一环路南一段 24 号四川大学望江校区内 In Sichuan University Wangjiang Campus, 24 Section 1, 1st Ring Road South, Wuhou District
98	彭镇老面坊 Old Flour Mill in Pengzhen Town	双流区彭镇永丰街 111-131 号 111-131 Yongfeng Street, Pengzhen Town, Shuangliu District

序号 Serial No.	名称 Name	位置 Location
99	友爱镇徐家大院老宅 Xu's Old Courtyard House in Youai Town	郫都区友爱镇徐家大院乡村酒店内 In Xu's Courtyard Rural Hotel, Youai Town, Pidu District
100	三道堰街道青杠树电影院 Qinggangshu Cinema on Sandaoyan Street	郫都区三道堰街道三堰村9组105号 No. 105, Group 9, Sanyan Village, Sandaoyan Sub-district, Pidu District
101	三道堰街道青杠树供销社 Qinggangshu Supply and Marketing Cooperative in Sandaoyan Sub-district	郫都区三道堰街道三堰村9组 Group 9, Sanyan Village, Sandaoyan Sub-district, Pidu District
102	石桥镇陕西会馆 Shaanxi Guild Hall in Shiqiao Town	简阳市石桥镇陕西街 Shaanxi Street, Shiqiao Town, Jianyang City
103	夹关镇解放渡槽 Liberation Aqueduct in Jiaguan Town	邛崃市夹关镇拴马村8、9组 Groups 8 and 9, Shuanma Village, Jiaguan Town, Qionglai City
104	临邛镇张白祠堂 Zhang's and Bai's Ancestral Shrine in Linqiong Town	邛崃市临邛镇北坛社区11组 Group 11, Beitan Community, Linqiong Town, Qionglai City
105	广兴镇刁氏宗祠 Diao's Ancestral Shrine in Guangxing Town	金堂县广兴镇广严寺社区3组 Group 3, Guangyansi Community, Guangxing Town, Jintang County
106	弥牟镇温氏宗祠 Wen's Ancestral Shrine in Mimou Town	青白江区弥牟镇火星社区16组 Group 16, Huoxing Community, Mimou Town, Qingbaijiang District
107	原金堂县县政府大门 Entrance of Former Jintang County Government	青白江区城厢镇槐树街社区西街10号 10 West Street, Huaishujie Community, Chengxiang Town, Qingbaijiang District
108	黄龙溪镇铁匠铺 Smithy in Huanglongxi Town	双流区黄龙溪镇复兴街41号 41 Fuxing Street, Huanglongxi Town, Shuangliu District
109	唐昌街道青春村刘家院子 Liu's Courtyard in Qingchun Village, Tangchang Sub-district	郫都区唐昌街道青春村1组 Group 1, Qingchun Village, Tangchang Sub-district, Pidu District
110	原四川省青城造纸厂厂房 Factory Building of Former Sichuan Qingcheng Paper Mill	都江堰市壹街区玉垒路51号 51 Yulei Road, Yijiequ Block, Dujiangyan City
111	道佐乡郭家大院 Guo's Grand Courtyard in Daozuo Township	邛崃市道佐乡寨沟村15组 Group 15, Zhaigou Village, Daozuo Township, Qionglai City
112	大同乡景沟廊桥 Jinggou Covered Bridge in Datong Township	邛崃市大同乡景沟村1组 Group 1, Jinggou Village, Datong Township, Qionglai City
113	悦来镇陈家祠堂 Chen's Ancestral Shrine in Yuelai Town	大邑县悦来镇丹凤村11组 Group 11, Danfeng Village, Yuelai Town, Daiyi County
114	兴义镇刘家院子 Liu's Courtyard in Xingyi Town	新津县兴义镇岷江社区菜棚子林盘内 In the Caipengzi Farmhouse Forest, Minjiang Community, Xingyi Town, Xinjin County
115	民航飞行学院陈列馆 Exhibition Hall of Civil Aviation Flight University of China	新津县花桥镇长春村5组 Group 5, Changchun Village, Huaqiao Town, Xinjin County
116	安西镇岳氏宗祠 Yue's Ancestral Shrine in Anxi Town	新津县安西镇月花村5组 Group 5, Yuehua Village, Anxi Town, Xinjin County
117	明月窑 Mingyue Kiln	蒲江县甘溪镇明月村12组 Group 12, Mingyue Village, Ganxi Town, Pujiang County
118	廖启清故居 Former Residence of Liao Qiqing	蒲江县寿安镇插旗山村6组 Group 6, Chaqishan Village, Shouan Town, Pujiang County

图书在版编目（CIP）数据

成都建筑·遗珠. Ⅰ / 成都市规划管理局，成都市城市建设档案馆编. -- 成都：四川美术出版社，2019.1
ISBN 978-7-5410-8470-6

Ⅰ. ①成… Ⅱ. ①成… ②成… Ⅲ. ①古建筑—成都—摄影集 Ⅳ. ① K928.71-64

中国版本图书馆 CIP 数据核字 (2018) 第 292059 号

成都建筑·遗珠 I

Chengdu Jianzhu Yizhu I

成都市规划管理局 成都市城市建设档案馆 编

出 品 人	马晓峰
责任编辑	汪青青
责任校对	田倩宇
出版发行	四川美术出版社
	成都市锦江区金石路 239 号 邮政编码：610000
成品尺寸	285mm × 285mm
印 张	22
图 片	298 幅
字 数	75 千字
版式设计	成都佳倍文化传播有限公司
印 刷	西南交通大学印刷厂
版 次	2018 年 12 月第 1 版
印 次	2018 年 12 月第 1 次印刷
印 数	2000
书 号	ISBN 978-7-5410-8470-6
定 价	398.00 元

成都建筑